CHOOSING
JOY

ALSO BY DR. RON LEE DAVIS

Ten Traits of a Healthy Parent

Healing Life's Hurts

Gold in the Making

Mentoring: The Strategy of the Master

Courage to Begin Again

A Forgiving God in an Unforgiving World

Mistreated

Becoming a Whole Person in a Broken World

A Time for Compassion

CHOOSING JOY

The pathway to a life of passion and purpose

DR. RON LEE DAVIS

amazon publishing

Published by: Independent Publishing

Published in the United States of America

ISBN: 978-0-578-70166-0

Lovingly dedicated to Van and Shay Davis,
My brother's two sons.
Van and Shay's hearts are
full of courage, kindness and joy.
Their dad, looking down on them from Eternity,
must be filled with pride and gratitude
for the men they have become.

❧

CONTENTS

PROLOGUE

It was a Monday evening. I had just flown to Dallas from my California home for the National Booksellers Association Convention. The first draft of my newest book was nearly completed, and I was planning to discuss this material with my publisher. As I walked into the Hyatt-Regency Hotel where an author's reception was being held, my mind was focused two states away, consumed with thoughts and prayers for my brother, Paul. For several weeks, he had been experiencing abdominal pains, and all the noninvasive medical tests had failed to yield a diagnosis. So now, at the same time I was in Dallas, my only sibling and best friend was undergoing exploratory surgery in a Denver hospital.

I met with my publisher at the reception. We chatted briefly, agreeing to meet for breakfast the next morning to discuss marketing strategy for the book. During the rest of the evening, I repeatedly left the reception, placing call after call from the lobby to the hospital in Denver. No one at the hospital could tell me anything about Paul's condition. I prayed and waited and continued calling until about 10:30 p.m. when a nurse finally told me Paul was out of surgery. She had orders, however, not to give out any other information over the phone.

More anxious than ever, I called Paul's home, hoping to speak with his wife, Jan. There was no answer. So next I called Marty Asbury, a good friend of Paul's. I knew Marty and his wife had stayed in the waiting room with my sister-in-law throughout Paul's surgery. "Jan just left a few minutes ago, but I can tell you what the doctors found," Marty told me. "Ron, Paul has cancer."

Cancer. The word penetrated like a knife. I tried to speak, but I couldn't. Instead, I found I was weeping. *I should have been there, I thought. I should have been with Jan and the boys when the doctors gave them the news.*

Marty went on, "It apparently began in the appendix, which is very rare, and it's spread to several other organs. The doctors think there's cancer in the liver, but they won't know for sure until the tests are in tomorrow. I'm sorry, Ron, but the doctors just aren't very optimistic. They only give Paul about six to twelve months."

My next call was to the airlines; I booked a 6 a.m. flight to Denver. I landed in Denver and took a cab to the hospital, arriving just a few minutes before Jan. She and I were both with Paul when the doctor came in and explained to him that he had an advanced cancer. Paul took the news with amazing steadiness and replied that he was ready to fight it any way he could. He asked simply, "What do we do now?"

In the weeks that followed, I made several more trips between Denver and my home in California. During those trips to Denver, I stayed day and night in Paul's hospital room while he underwent chemotherapy immediately after his completion of five weeks of radiation treatments. During those difficult days and long nights, whenever the pain and nausea of the chemotherapy would subside, Paul and I had opportunities to talk. We reminisced about growing up together in a small town in Iowa; and we talked of life and death and how Paul's faith in Christ was carrying him through this crisis. He shared very openly with me his fears regarding the future and his concerns for his wife and two young sons should this cancer take his life. We wept and prayed together many times, and I never felt closer to Paul than I did in those hours.

During those weeks, I watched Paul — who for over twenty years had been a coach to hundreds of young men, conducting basketball clinics around the country, active in the Fellowship of Christian Athletes — as he reached out from his hospital bed to touch the lives of young men whom he had already influenced powerfully for Christ. I saw tears streaming down the lean, tanned faces of rugged athletes as they dropped all their "macho" pretenses, and wept openly at Paul's bedside.

It was only two months after Paul's cancer was first diagnosed that he suddenly began to develop serious complications. When we received the news, my mother flew to Denver from Iowa, and I again flew back from California. In his hospital room, my mother was able to tell Paul how much she loved him and what a wonderful son he'd been. I stayed through that night beside Paul's bed as he alternated between sleep and wakefulness. When he was awake, we talked, sharing thoughts and memories and prayers. During those long midnight hours in that darkened hospital room, Paul was as close to God as I had ever seen him.

At 8:00 a.m. the next morning, Jan and I hugged him and prayed with him as he was wheeled down the hallway to surgery. We stopped at the door that led to the operating room, and I kissed Paul on the neck, and told him I loved him. He told me that he loved me. Then he and Jan had a few precious moments together, and at last Paul was taken into surgery. That was the last conversation Jan and I had with Paul in this life. Despite the doctor's best efforts, the surgery was unable to extend Paul's life any further. The next morning, my brother — and closest friend — passed from this life into eternity.

Through the years, I have come to realize that time will never fully heal this sorrow I feel for the loss of my brother. I expect the grief I feel for Paul to recur again and again as long as I live — and that's as it should be. When we love someone deeply, it hurts us deeply to try to let him or her go. As Queen Elizabeth II wrote eloquently, *"Grief is the price we pay for love."*

Still, despite the sorrow, the unanswered questions, and the trials and tears that continue in my life, I choose joy.

This book is about the reality that with the help of our loving God, we can choose joy even in the midst of life's greatest trials.

Scripture promises that we can actually have joy no matter how difficult our circumstances. *"Consider it all joy, my brethren, when you encounter various trials,"* says James 1:2 (NASB). Yet joy is usually the last thing we think of as we face our trials — and understandably so. The first thing that occurs to us in the hard places of life is not joy, but *"Why me? Why this? Why now?"* When we're hurting, we have some questions to ask God — and God accepts our questions. He understands our heartaches.

However, there comes a time when we need to cognitively reframe our thinking so that we can move beyond our questions. In the chapters ahead, we will discover together how we can choose joy through all the seasons of life.

Over twenty-five years ago, I embarked upon a research project focusing on one primary topic. My probing question was: What are the ingredients that could enable a person to experience an authentically joyful life and healthy aging process? I read over 100 books on various components of joyful living, and interacted with various psychologists, authors, sociologists, physicians, theologians, nutritional scientists, exercise physiologists, gerontologists and research technologists. Many of my conclusions in this book are drawn from this long-term exploration.

Yet, this book is not written from some theological or psychological ivory tower, far removed from hard realities of life. I have buried all of my beloved family of origin now, lived with seven years of daily chronic pain, cared for my critically ill daughter who was in isolation for one year, written over one hundred eulogies for loved ones from age 7 to 97 who have transitioned from this life into Eternity, cared for both the ill and the unemployed during the COVID-19 pandemic, and battled through seasons of doubt and discouragement. Still, I have discovered again and again throughout my life pilgrimage that we can all have the compassionate guidance of a God who longs to come alongside us through our journey. Join me in the pages ahead as we discover that we can, with authenticity, learn to choose joy.

Chapter 1

CHOOSING JOY

While I was serving as a youth pastor for ten years at a wonderful church in Minneapolis, I kept only one piece of paper underneath the glass on my office desk. Through the years, while the words on the page faded, I continued to read them, and they helped shape my life:

"Do you act or react? I was accompanying a friend to a news stand recently. Upon approaching the news stand, I noted that the man selling papers was openly sullen and cantankerous. I then noticed that my friend was kind and cordial in every way in dealing with the man. As we walked away from the news stand, I asked, 'Is that fellow always so mean?' 'Yes, unfortunately he is', my friend answered. And I persisted, 'And you are always so nice to him?' 'Well, yes. I guess I am', replied my friend. 'Why?', I asked. He responded, 'Because I don't want him, or anyone else, to decide for me how I am going to act. I need to decide how I am going to act. In my life, I want to act, not react.' That was one of the most important lessons of my life — to learn to act, not react to life's circumstances." - Sydney Harris, reflecting on the reality that we have the power to choose our own attitude.

Major Harold Kushner, an army medical officer held by the Viet Cong for a period of five years in the 1970's, writes about attitude choice. He tells us the tragic story of one man who made a change in his choice of attitude, and how this change in attitude would ultimately lead to a change from life to death. He writes these words:

Among the prisoners in the P.O.W. camp was a strong, young marine, 24 years old, who had already survived two years of prison camp life in good health. Part of the reason for this was that the camp commander had promised to release this young man if he cooperated. Since this had been done before with others, the Marine turned into a model P.O.W. and leader of the camp reform group.

As time passed, the marine gradually realized that his captors had lied to him. When the full realization of this reality took hold, the young Marine made an atti-tude choice. He now refused to do all work, he reject-ed all offers of food and encouragement, and he simp-ly lay on his cot. In a matter of weeks, he died."

Dr. Martin Seligman, a brilliant cognitive therapist and pioneer of the positive psychology movement in this country, writes, *"Clearly, the marine's death can only be attributed to his change of attitude."*

A friend of mine is a C.S. Lewis scholar. He has read every book and article ever written by the late C.S. Lewis, the prolific Christian author and lay theologian. Some time ago in a personal letter to me, my friend wrote these words,

"C.S. Lewis' life has always had a greater impact on me than his writings, as powerful as they were. For 30 years, he was blackballed by the Oxford Administra-tors and fellow staff from obtaining a full professor-ship, where – despite his brilliance — he retained the title of Tutor. Fueled by his gifts and his passion for Christ, he persevered through ridicule and continued to write and speak. C.S. Lewis' greatest works emerged out of those years of greatest persecution. Ron, as you probably know, he was openly criticized and opposed by his peers for spending all his energy on Christian writing. Yet, in the world outside Oxford, his views and ideas impacted so many for Christ. His beloved book, The Screwtape Letters, appeared in 1943 at the apex of the criticism and opposition against him. On top of all of this were his personal

losses: his mother's death, the rejection by his father,
the death of his best army companion, the sudden death
of his life-long friend, Charles Williams in 1945 – and
then the agonizing death of his new bride, Joy Da-
vidman. C.S. Lewis, in the midst of a world of opposi-
tion and tragedy, continued to live his life choosing an
attitude of joy."

It is extremely difficult to overemphasize the crucial importance of the attitude choice we make in our daily lives as we discover a life of joy and gratitude. Indeed, this choice can have profound implications for both the health and length of our lives and the quality of our family life together.

Consider, for example, a recent study that researched 4,500 widowers for a period of years after the death of their spouses. The study compared these 4,500 widowers with 4,500 other men of similar ages and health. The conclusion was that the widowers had a 41% higher mortality rate. Why? The study concluded that the primary cause was *"because of a profound change in attitude toward life and their future."*

In Philippians 2:5 we read, *"Your attitude should be the same as Christ Jesus."* What was the attitude of Christ Jesus? As we scan the earthly ministry of Christ, was it not in large measure an attitude of joy as He pointed all of us to a lifestyle whereby we intentionally view all of life with hearts of gratitude?

I have often said to my family that one clear expectation they should have of me is that I would be consistently modeling a positive and joyful attitude toward the challenges of daily life. Further, I understand that I am to be *reframing* the difficulties of life with my children and grandchildren so that they might view these challenges from a positive and joyful perspective. In point of fact, one of the primary responsibilities of every parent is to help his or her child *reframe* the various obstacles that are a part of all our lives.

Years ago, at a National Christian Booksellers Convention, I had the privilege of meeting best-selling Christian author Joni Erickson Tada. Some of you may remember her story:

"It was the summer of 1967. On a barge about 50 yards from the shore, an attractive, vibrant young woman dived into the murky water of The Chesapeake Bay. The water level was more shallow than Joni had expected, and her head hit a rock. She became immediately paralyzed from the neck down. No more sports cars, no more horseback rides, no more volleyball on the beach. She recalls, "I was devastated. My life had been so full. I had been involved in as many school activities as I could squeeze in, and suddenly I found myself alone – all alone – just a limp body between two sheets. My hobbies and possessions were meaningless to me now. Those beautiful horses in the barn who I used to trick ride – standing on their shoulders – I would never ride them again. I could not even feed myself. I could sleep and breathe. Everything else was done for me. I was locked into a harness in my bed and required to turn my face to the floor to keep from getting bed sores. My tears fell from my eyes and made designs on the floor. Gradually, with God's help, my attitude began to change. I now awoke every day grateful for what God had given me. It took me some time to admit it, but God had proven to me that I, too, can have a full life."

Joni has led a rich, full and meaningful life of joy and gratitude, reaching thousands with Christ's love.

Sydney Harris, C.S. Lewis, Joni Erickson Tada: what do all these diverse individuals have in common? All of them, at some point in their lives, made an attitude choice that led them on a journey toward a life of joy and gratitude

May that reality be true for all of us.

Chapter 2

CHOOSING JOY BY DISCOVERING SPIRITUAL AND EMOTIONAL HEALTH

Sometime ago, I blocked out several months to research only one question: *What are the ingredients that would enable a Christian to become spiritually and emotionally healthy?* Studying and praying at my ocean side apartment in Santa Barbara, I poured over scripture and books by Christian theologians, psychologists, sociologists and philosophers.

At the end of this pilgrimage, I synthesized all of my conclusions and realized that six key questions could guide us through a process of candid self-evaluation as we seek to discover where we may need to grow in our walk with Christ.

1.   Do I have two or three deep, authentic friendships?

Outside of our own family, do I have two or three deep, authentic friendships? The research overwhelmingly indicates that people who age joyfully have a social network of at least two to three genuine, heart-felt friends. These are the type of friends where I know deeply in my heart that they care more about my *character* than my *comfort.*

Dr. David Lynch in his excellent book, *The Broken Heart*, provides significant research that demonstrates that when we choose *isolation* rather than reaching out in deep, bonding, loving friendships, then when illness strikes, there is *ten times* the likelihood that the illness will become more severe.

Dr. Dean Ornish in his excellent book, *"Love and Survival"*, verified after extensive research that people without two to three close friends have *five times* the likelihood of premature death.

There is a beautiful verse tucked away in the Old Testament that reads simply, *"David loved Jonathan, and their souls were knit together"* (I Samuel 18:1) My brother Paul and I shared this as our life verse.

Reflect with me for a moment. Is there a name you could put in place of Jonathan, along with your name, where before God in a moment of self-evaluation, you could say: "Yes, I have a friend with such a depth of love that our souls are knit together."?

Before his death, my life-long friend, Dr. Pedro Garcia wrote a letter to me containing this excerpt:

> *"I have had many acquaintances in my lifetime. However, true friendship, like the one we share, comes only rarely. We are older now, but our hearts are still childlike, and I know our hearts will always have room for each other. Many things have happened to us, but neither years nor miles can ever change our love for each other. Henry Wadsworth Longfellow wrote 'And the song from beginning to the end, I have found in the heart of a friend.' I love you."*

Do I have two or three deep, authentic friendships?

2. Do I freely admit mistakes, genuinely ask forgiveness from those I have hurt, and offer forgiveness to all?

In many psychiatric wards and Christian treatment centers for addiction, there is one well-placed sign over the entryway to the facility that asks simply, *"Do You Want to be Right or Well?"*

Research indicates conclusively that many of us, especially men, are raised from childhood to try very hard to always be right, to justify ourselves, to view conflict as an interpersonal activity that we need to *win*. Accordingly, it can be very difficult for many adults, even after they come to Christ, to adopt a posture of becoming non-defensive. Ultimately, God yearns for all of us to find it less and less difficult to say these twelve words: *"I am sorry. Please forgive me. I was wrong. I love you."*

Living in forgiveness is foundational to joyful spiritual and emotional health - both the *asking* and the *granting* of forgiveness. I've been alive long enough to know three sets of parents who were able to forgive the person who took their child's life. I've been alive long enough to know one individual who drove many miles to a cemetery where her dad was buried.

There, she knelt down beside her dad's tombstone and said aloud these words addressed to her father who had consistently physically and verbally abused her for years: "Dad, from this day forward you will receive nothing but *unconditional love* from me. *I forgive you.*"

Do I freely admit mistakes, genuinely ask forgiveness from those whom I have hurt, and offer forgiveness to all?

3. Do I take full and complete responsibility for my life?

Put another way, have I stopped blaming others for my problems? By way of recent cultural and historical perspective, a growing number of sociologists and psychologists are verifying that we are becoming a society of victims. As a culture, we are increasingly adopting a mentality — and teaching our children to adopt a mentality— that encourages that if anything goes wrong, we are victims who somehow, some way can find someone else to blame. This cultural mentality, so prevalent in current American thought patterns, stands in diametric opposition to the call of Christ upon our lives.

The psychologist Carl Rogers wrote years ago:

"There is only one person whom I have no hope for in terms of ever coming to spiritual and emotional healing - that is the person who continually blames others for his problems."

For many years, author John Powell had a sign placed on the top of his bathroom mirror so that it would be the first statement he would read each day: *"You are now looking at the face of the person who is responsible for your joy today."*

One Christian psychologist puts it this way: *"Growth begins where blaming ends."*

Do I take full and complete responsibility for my life?

4. Do I live life as a joyful spiritual adventure, constantly seeking new opportunities to serve Christ and others?

An insightful scripture study to undertake would be to begin in the book of Genesis and work our way through the New Testament, and observe how many of the great Biblical characters viewed their lives as a passionate adventure to be lived for God until they went one day to be with Him.

Think with me, for example, of Joseph and Paul. These men, even in their prison years, kept asking, in essence, "What new grand adventure is God now calling me to in this jail cell?"

Do we all realize that in scripture we find no concept of what we call today, "retirement"? It is an absolutely foreign concept in the Bible. We may conclude our work in some vocation or career, but we never "retire" from asking the question: *"What new adventure are you calling me to embark upon, Loving God, in making a difference in your kingdom agenda here on earth?"* That process never ends until God calls us Home.

One Christian psychologist writes: *"An inordinate need for safety is a sign of emotional illness."* Was this not, in part, what Jesus was driving at when he said as recorded in all four of the Gospels: *"Whoever would save his life will lose it. But whoever would lose his life for my sake, will find it."* (Mathew 16:25)

Helen Keller, author, teacher and the first deaf and blind person to earn a bachelor of arts degree in the United States, put it succinctly when she said, *"Life is either a daring adventure or it is nothing at all."*

Sociologists tell us that one common characteristic found in the three communities in the world where the average life span hovers around age 100 is: *"These villagers live their lives actively as a joyful adventure, continuing to work and serve and love their families and friends well into their latter 90's. In all three villages, the word 'retirement' is not in their vocabulary. They literally did not under-stand the word."*

Do I live life as a joyful spiritual adventure, constantly seeking new opportunities to serve Christ and others?

5. Do people feel valued whenever they are around me?

Christian psychological research indicates that people who have to constantly be at the center of attention have this relational style due to deep-seeded insecurity and low self-esteem. Often, when driving to meet a new friend for tea or lunch, I'll pray aloud in the car, "Loving God, help me to remember it's more important to be *interested* than to be *interesting*. Help me to be more of an *asker* than a *teller*. Help me to show a genuine and heartfelt interest in this new friend and *his/her* needs."

Years ago, I flew into Los Angeles to be interviewed at a Christian television station upon the release of a new book. As I arrived, a kind and gentle SUV driver named Harold picked me up at the airport to drive me to the studio. As we rode along together, I asked Harold about his life. He proceeded to share with me his amazing testimony. At one time deeply addicted to drugs and alcohol, Harold had lost his family and his job. But then Harold met God. Through a dramatic conversion, Harold gave his life to Christ, was restored and fully reconciled with his family, and now was working for a Christian ministry.

As we arrived at the television station, I said, "What a wonderful story, Harold. You must enjoy sharing it with many people as you drive back and forth between the airport and studio."

"Oh," replied Harold, "You are the first one who ever asked. The folks I pick up are either telling me about their new book or quietly preparing for their interview."

"How long have you worked as a driver for the station?" I asked.

"Nine years", was Harold's sad reply.

In the 25th Chapter of Matthew, there is a beautiful passage where we read that whenever we joyfully minister to another person, we are ministering to Christ in some way that we may not fully understand until eternity.

Do people feel *valued* around us, or are we more interested in telling *our* story?

6. Do I have the courage to choose joy?

Nehemiah 8:10 reads: *"The joy of the Lord is my strength."* Proverbs 17:22 reads, *"A joyful heart is good medicine."*

Do we realize that these two verses have been scientifically proven to be true? Do we realize that when we choose to withdraw from a life of joy, our immune system is weakened? Do we realize that when we choose joy, we now know that chemicals are released in the human body that actually give us *strength*?

*"The **joy** of the Lord is my strength."* (Nehemiah 8:10)

Norman Cousins, in his excellent book, *The Anatomy of An Illness,* wrote these words:

> *"Scientific research has established the existence of endorphins in the brain. Endorphins are the body's own anesthetic and relaxant. Endorphins help human beings to sustain in the midst of pain. There is now evidence to support the conviction that endorphins are released in the body primarily through experiences of joy."*

Perhaps some of you are reading about this sixth question thinking, "Ron, that's easy for you to write about, but you're not in the situation I'm facing. You simply don't know what I'm going through this week." Certainly, any writer should know this potential criticism lurks when this theme is addressed.

In this regard, I'm reminded of an old friend of mine, Tim Hansel.

Tim Hansel was a gifted Christian leader, speaker and author. For many years Tim lived in daily, constant, chronic, severe pain, caused from breaking his back in an accident. Several years ago, Tim was speaking to a large gathering on the topic of Choosing Joy. After he had concluded his teaching, a woman approached him and asked, "Do you mean to suggest that *I'm* supposed to choose *joy*? My only son, my only child, was killed three weeks ago in an automobile accident and you are telling me to choose *joy*?" Tim Hansel, with tears welling up in his eyes, replied tenderly, "I'm so, so sorry. Forgive me if I said anything in my talk to offend or hurt you. I believe you need to take *all the time you need* to work through the grieving process." And then Tim paused for a moment, gently put his arm on the woman's shoulder, and said, "But I also believe that there will come a time in your grieving process where God is going to want to enable you with His Holy Spirit to give you the *courage* to choose *joy*. It may only be for two or three minutes at first, but He does want you to choose joy. I really believe God wants that, and you know, *I'll bet your son would want that, too.* "

1. Do I have two or three deep, authentic friendships?
2. Do I freely admit mistakes, genuinely ask forgiveness from those I have hurt, and offer forgiveness to all?
3. Do I take full and complete responsibility for my life?
4. Do I live life as a joyful, spiritual adventure, constantly seeking new opportunities to serve Christ and others?
5. Do people feel valued whenever they are around me?
6. Do I have the courage to choose joy?

I believe that if we can say a resounding "yes" to these six questions, we are well on our way to joyful spiritual and emotional wholeness in Christ.

Chapter 3

CHOOSING JOY AS WE LIVE OUT OUR LIVES FOR GOD'S GOOD

Elizabeth Hansen grew up in love with God, and at the age of seven, felt God's call to the mission field. She graduated from Bible College, received her medical training, and willingly accepted her first assignment to a country in Central Africa where political turmoil had led to military unrest.

One night a group of rebels came into the clinic where Elizabeth Hansen served as a nurse, and after destroying her medical supplies, they came into the hut where Elizabeth was sleeping, where they beat, abused and raped her.

As Elizabeth was enduring this humiliation on the dirt floor of her hut, she cried out, "God, why? I gave my life to you. I followed your call to Africa. Why are you allowing this to happen to me?" Elizabeth later said it was as if God spoke to her in that moment and said, *"Elizabeth, when you gave me your life, you gave me your heart. When you gave me your life, you gave me your mind. And, when you gave me your life, you gave me your body. They're not just doing this to you. I am here with you. Even in this."*

Several months later, Elizabeth was on furlough in the United States. One day she was giving a lecture on a technical medical topic at a local college. In the middle of her lecture, she noticed two girls who seemed younger than the other students in the class. Elizabeth began to sense the nudging from God to interrupt her lecture, and tell her story of her humiliation that night in Africa. Elizabeth wrestled with God over this prodding from His Spirit. She had never shared her story before. Why now? Finally, she relented, and shared the story of her abuse and rape. After sharing her story, she completed her lecture and dismissed the class.

After all the students had filed out, the two young girls remained in the classroom. The older of the two approached Elizabeth and said, "We weren't even supposed to be in the classroom. We came to another meeting, and entered this room by mistake, and then were too embarrassed to leave. My sister, who is sitting over there, was raped two months ago in a park near our house, and since then, she has not said one word to me, to mom and dad, to our pastor, to her counselor."

Elizabeth Hansen looked over into the eyes of the 13-year old girl. The young girl gazed into the eyes of Elizabeth — and then ran into her arms. For the next hour, Elizabeth listened to the young girl as she shared the details of her terrible ordeal. After an hour of sharing, Elizabeth gently, tenderly led this girl to Christ. Today this teenage girl has grown into a woman actively serving Christ in the ministry.

Elizabeth Hansen being abused in Africa was not a good thing, but God's good came from it. We read of God's good in Romans 8:28-29, *"We know that in everything God works for good for those who love Him, who are called according to His purpose. For those whom He foreknew, He also predestined to be conformed to the image of his Son, in order that He might be the first-born among many brethren."*

Romans 8:28 could be described as both the most beloved, and the most misunderstood verse in the Bible.

Biblical scholar F. F. Bruce suggests that the subject of the sentence in Romans 8:28 is the word *"God"*. If the subject of the sentence is the word "God", then the word "good" must first of all refer to God, rather than to you and me. Scores of Greek New Testament scholars agree with F. F. Bruce on this point.

To understand this crucial insight is to understand Romans 8:28 in a whole new and deeper way for many of us. The wonderful assurance of this verse is that God is at work for *His ultimate good* in our lives, if we truly love Him.

Many translations and paraphrases of Romans 8:28 miss the mark in terms of what the Apostle Paul is driving at in His verse. For example, one popular paraphrase reads, "We know that *all* that happens to us is working for *our* good." This paraphrase misses the mark on two levels:

- First, not every single thing that happens to us in our lives is good. Many events, in and of themselves, will not be good. Often, they will be heartbreaking and tragic. To pretend that they are good, by either denying our emotions or falsely teaching others that every single event in life is good, is a perversion of the Gospel. Rather, the promise of Romans 8:28 as we wrestle with the Greek text, is that all things — when they have been woven and weaved together — can bring forth good.
- Second, this good is not necessarily our own immediate good as we will understand it in this lifetime. No, this good is first of all *God's good* — and the furtherance of His Kingdom here on earth.

For many years, Dr. E. C. Caldwell served as the Professor of New Testament at Union Theological Seminary in Richmond, Virginia. One day, Dr. Caldwell was completing his lecture from Romans, and giving the assignment for the next class session with some brief comments as to what to look for and what to avoid in the text. He said, "For tomorrow, I want you to study Romans 8:28-39. Look closely at the passage. In verse 28, notice in the text that it does not say *every single thing* in life is good. No, in everything, God's good. The emphasis is always on *God*."

Then, according to his students, Dr. Caldwell paused for a moment, took off his glasses and in a very uncharacteristic fashion, said, "Always remember, whatever happens in your life, whatever happens in your ministry, Romans 8:28 still holds true."

That afternoon, Dr. Caldwell and his wife were out for a leisurely drive in their car when a Richmond train hit them at a crossing. Dr. Caldwell's wife was killed instantly. Dr. Caldwell was critically injured, and permanently crippled.

After a prolonged convalescence, Dr. Caldwell returned to his class with aid of a cane. All in the class remembered their last time together, and what Dr. Caldwell had said. They wondered what he would say now. Dr. Caldwell limped in from the back of the classroom after everyone was seated, and slowly made his way to the front where he turned and said, "Romans 8:28 still holds true! One day we shall see God's good coming even from this. Even from this."

C. S. Lewis had a hunch regarding what would be the most frequently spoken word in Heaven. C. S. Lewis' conjecture was that the most frequently spoken word in Heaven would be, ***"Oh!"*** As in *"Oh, now I understand." "Oh, now I see more clearly." "Oh, now I perceive why my brother Paul was taken at such a young age." "And, those trials and heartaches I faced, oh, now I understand more clearly what I once could only see so dimly."*

We have the wonderful certainty that if we love God, and are seeking daily to leave a legacy for God, then one day in eternity we shall look back on all the events of our lives, when they have been woven and weaved together, and say a magnificent, *"Oh!"*

In Romans 8:29, we see the reason for God's good being worked out in our lives: *"For those whom he foreknew, he also predestined **to become conformed into the image of Christ."*** The *reason* for the promise of Romans 8:28 is found in Romans 8:29. God has made a decision ahead of time about every one of us. The decision he has made about us is that we all should gradually become more and more like Christ. The central goal for the Christian is that he or she is seeking in partnership with our living God to become more like Christ.

Sometimes we become more like Christ through a trial or heartache.

Years ago, all-star baseball player Dave Dravecky read one of my books when he was going through a trial in his life, and we began to correspond with each other. As some of you avid baseball fans may remember, San Francisco Giants pitcher Dave Dravecky had his left arm amputated due to a malignant tumor. Shortly after his surgery,

Dave wrote this note to my daughter, Rachael.

"Rachael, I have come to realize that God uses trials and sufferings in our life to draw us closer to Him, and help us become more conformed into the image of Jesus (Romans 8:29). With the events that have taken place over the past months, II Corinthians 4:16-18 have become special verses in my life:

> '*For we do not lose heart, for though outwardly we are wasting away, yet inwardly we are being renewed every day. For our light and momentary troubles are achieving for us an eternal glory that far outweighs them all. So we fix our eyes not on what is seen, but on what is unseen. For what is seen is temporal – but what is unseen is eternal.*'"

Dave Dravecky having cancer was not a good thing. But in all sorts of ways, God's good has come from it, even to this very day.

Before his death, I was privileged to forge out a friendship with a dynamic evangelist named Tom Skinner. On one occasion, Tom told me about a friend of his named Don. Don noticed one day that he had a growth developing on his left ear. He made an appointment with his family doctor who told him, "There's a tumor there and it might be malignant. I'll have a specialist take some tests today."

Don went home that evening, and was doing his daily Bible study when he turned to Romans 8:28. As he was studying the passage with a helpful commentary, he realized in the flow of the text what the familiar verse was really saying: *If Don loved God and made himself available to God, then God's ultimate good would be accomplished in his life, whether it would be for his immediate good or not.*

So after reading Romans 8:28, he knelt down beside his bed and prayed this prayer: *"Heavenly Father, I know that through your son Jesus Christ you are The Great Physician. I know that you can heal me of this tumor."* Most of us would perhaps have stopped our prayer right there, but Don went on to pray, *"But, God, if on the other hand you can get more good out of my life, more of Your good out of my life, by my having cancer, then I readily accept the cancer."*

The next day the results of the test were complete. Don had a malignant tumor, and was admitted into the hospital. The surgeon would have to remove Don's ear.

The very first week Don was in the hospital, his positive, winsome, loving response to his surgery touched the heart of his roommate so deeply that his new roommate decided to follow the same Christ Don followed. Today, Don's roommate is a missionary in South America, who has ministered to the poorest of the poor with the love of God.

As Don recuperated from his surgery, he became acquainted with a nurse's aide in the hospital, and led her to Christ. The aide then felt led by God to go to medical school and became a nurse, ministering to the spiritual and physical needs of her many patients.

During his stay in the hospital, Don built a relationship with a man down the hallway who was one of the most influential businessmen in America. Through Don's example in the midst of his battle with cancer, he led that businessman to Christ, who in turn has led scores of men around the country to Christ through the National Christian Businessmen Association.

Today, Don wears one artificial left ear. He wears it for God's good. If you ask him if he would exchange that artificial left ear for normal hearing again, he says, "Not on your life. Because I was willing to live out my life for God's good, I know that today there are literally hundreds of people in North America and South America who have been touched with the love of Christ."

I believe with all my heart that you and I can have the joyful assurance from Romans 8:28-29 that one day in Eternity we shall be able to look back and say, *"Oh, now I see how everything woven and weaved together was used for Your good and the furtherance of Your kingdom because I loved you."*

Chapter 4

CHOOSING JOY AS WE STAND BY THE BROKEN-HEARTED

Several years ago, I received a call from my friend Edie Bizot at 1:30 a.m. Edie and her husband, Dave, had been lovingly caring for their eight-year-old son Kevin as he courageously battled cancer.

"I don't think Kevin will be with us much longer," she said. Her voice, though controlled, was eloquent with emotion and exhaustion. "He didn't come through the surgery too well, Ron, and he's in a coma. They've put him on a respirator and he's barely breathing. Could you come?"

I drove to the hospital where Kevin was fighting for his life and spent the rest of the night and most of the next day with Dave and Edie. I watched this father and mother lovingly care for their little boy during the last hours of his life. I thought about how kind and happy little Kevin was, and how much this beloved boy — like his father and mother — loved God.

The nurses gently placed Kevin in his father's arms, despite the monitors and IV tubes that were attached to him. Dave rocked Kevin for a long time as I talked with Edie. "Kevin was just on loan to us, Ron," she said softly. "For however long we have them, our children are just on loan to us. We care for them and love them. And when the time comes, we give them back to our heavenly Father. We know that Kevin belongs to God."

Then, it was Edie's turn to hold Kevin. She rocked him, stroked his face, and whispered to him. Dave said to me, "Edie and I don't want Kevin to be snatched from us. We want to offer him back to God." So we placed our hands on this precious little boy and gave him back to God. We thanked God for Kevin's eight beautiful years of life.

A short time later, little Kevin left his parents' arms and was lifted into the arms of his loving Father.

During our long vigil together that day long ago, I often struggled with what to say to this young couple. Words of guidance escaped me. I had no articulate speech of peace and consolation. It felt as though all I could do was weep with them. It felt as though all I could do was *stand by*.

Stand by – these two words have almost always had a negative connotation in our society today. We've all heard about violent crimes committed within view of respectable citizens who do nothing but stand by. You may have gone through the uneasy experience of trying to book a seat on a plane, only to be listed as a standby passenger. Your television screen suddenly goes blank in the fourth quarter of an NFL game; in dismay you read the words, "PLEASE STAND BY." Or perhaps you've been at the scene of some small household disaster — such as a bowl of oatmeal that fell to the floor and shattered — and your spouse said to you, "Don't just stand by and watch! *Do* something!"

To stand by seems to suggest helplessness, inactivity, or apathy. However, I urge you to see the act of *standing by* in a new light, as a positive form of the ministry of healing and consolation.

Often in the Scriptures we see that God encouraged and emboldened His people with the simple promise, "I am *standing by you*." Over and over again throughout the Old and New Testament, God comforts us with the loving promise of His Presence.

In his beautiful, tragic book, *Death be Not Proud*, John Gunther tells of the agony of having to stand by and watch the suffering of his little son Johnny. He writes:

> *"During Johnny's long illness, I prayed continually to God. Naturally, God was always there. He sat beside us during the doctor's consultation, as we waited the long vigils outside the operating room, as we rejoiced in the miracle of a brief recovery, as we agonized when hope ebbed away and the doctors confessed there was no longer anything they could do. They were helpless and we were helpless. But God in His*

infinite wisdom, God in His mercy and loving kind-
ness, God in all of His omnipotence in our hour of
need, was standing by us."

Scripture affirms that God often wants to use us as a representative of His love to the brokenhearted. Not everyone can be a teacher or a choir director or a youth leader. But everyone can perform the ministry of *standing by* — of being *compassionately present.*

I often am reminded in the midst of these devastating circumstances of the words of that gifted Christian author, Joe Bayly. Bayly was familiar with this level of heartache, having lost three children – two as teenagers and one as a five year old – to three distinct illnesses. He vulnerably writes these words after the death of his third boy:

> *"I was sitting, torn by grief. Someone came and talked to me of God's dealings, of why it happened, of hope beyond the grave. He talked constantly; he said things I knew were true. I was unmoved, except to wish he'd go away. He finally did.*
>
> *And then another man came and sat beside me for an hour or more, listened when I said something, answered briefly, prayed simply, left. I was moved. I was comforted. I hated to see him go.*
>
> *An arm about the shoulder, a firm grip of the hand, a kiss: these are the proofs that grief needs, not logical reasoning."*

As we stand by hurting family members and friends in the days ahead, it is good to remember that very often our simple presence without words is often the greatest expression of love.

In this regard, it generally is not helpful to glibly utter that familiar cliché, "Time will heal it all." For time very often does NOT heal it all, as the wound turns into a scar that will never fully heal.

Christian author Henri Nouwen wrote these words to his grieving father after the death of his wife.

> *"Real grief is not healed by time. It is false to think that the passing of time will slowly make us forget her and take away our pain. I really want to console you in this letter, dad, but not by suggesting that time will take away your pain, and that in one, two or three more years you will not miss her anymore. I would not only be telling a lie, I would be diminishing the importance of mother's life and underestimating the depth of your love for her, shared together for 47 years. If time does anything, it deepens our grief. The longer we live, the more fully we become aware of who she was for us, and the more intimately we experience what her love meant to us."* - From A Letter of Consolation

As we *stand by* compassionately, God often leads us to offer *practical encouragement* to the grieving friend. What do we say to someone who is hurting, depressed, lonely? Often one of the most spiritually mature and helpful things to say is: "Let's go have lunch together." "Let's walk by the lake together." Lots of deeply committed, well-meaning Christians have the tendency to quote from a sermon or a book some lofty, abstract thought or idea to a heartbroken friend. But often what is needed most is just some very practical encouragement. When I recall the storms that have entered my life, so often the questions that have helped me the most have come from loving Christian friends who have asked:

- "Can we bring over dinner tonight? It's one less concern your family needs to worry about right now."

- "Can I lead our board meeting in your place tonight? Why don't you take the evening off and listen to your favorite music or play with the grandchildren."

- "I'm not a counselor, but I'm a pretty good listener. Would you want to meet at the coffee shop for an hour and just share with me how you're holding up?"

Practical encouragement.

On two occasions, I had the opportunity to meet David Rothenburg and his mother, Marie. You may remember the story of David Rothenburg. Years ago, when David was only eight years old, his father had taken his young son to Disneyland. David's mother and father were separated, and Mr. Rothbenburg was battling depression. Once David and his father arrived in Anaheim, it began to rain. The rare Southern California storm lasted several days and was so severe that Disneyland remained closed all week. As the days and nights slowly passed, the emotionally broken father became more and more despondent in the hotel room with his young boy. Finally, in an act of great cruelty, he set the room on fire with his son lying in the hotel bed. Amazingly, the little boy survived – although his body was badly burned from head to toe.

Ken and Judy Curtis, a married couple living in Southern California, heard the news of this tragedy on their car radio. They did not know David or his mother, Marie, who had by now flown to Los Angeles to be with her suffering son. But their Christian faith and love motivated them to reach out to this mother and son with a ministry of *practical encouragement*. Marie wrote these words about one of her first visits to the hospital in her excellent book, *David* (Fleming H. Revell publishing). (Comments in parenthesis are my reflections):

> *"My son, Davie, was listening to a record about David and Goliath. As I came into his room that evening,*

I noticed that one of his ears had now fallen off. What next could happen to my little boy? He had lost all of his hair, his nose was burned, his face was burned, all of his body was burned and now one of his ears had fallen off. With tears streaming down my face, I found my way to the car I had borrowed from Ken and Judy." (Note the ministry of practical encouragement. The Curtis's loaned Marie their car.)

"I made my way up and down those strange Los Angeles streets to my room in Ken and Judy's home." (Practical Encouragement: Ken and Judy had opened their home to Marie who lived on the East coast and had no place to stay in Los Angeles.) *'Just come and live with us while your son is in the hospital,' Judy said. Ken and Judy were waiting there for me as I ran in angry and sobbing. Ken pulled out a chair for me, and Judy had a cup of tea waiting."* (Practical Encouragement) *"And then they just sat there with me, comforting me, waiting with me, weeping with me through the entire night."* (Practical Encouragement.)

Through Ken and Judy's ministry of practical encouragement, David and Marie were sustained in their darkest hours. They yielded their lives to the same Christ Ken and Judy Curtis followed.

Christian author Henri Nouwen stood by literally thousands of heartbroken people throughout his life. Shortly before he died, he wrote: *"Compassion asks us to go where it hurts, to enter into the place of pain, to share in brokenness, fear, confusion and anguish. Compassion challenges us to cry out with those in misery, to mourn with those who are lonely, to weep with those in tears. Compassion requires the full immersion of our whole selves into the lives of the brokenhearted."*

Two ways we honor these words are by quietly *standing by* the grieving and gently offering them *practical encouragement.* As we perform these two loving expressions of ministry, we enable our grieving friends to begin to move to a place where they can one day once again choose joy.

Chapter 5

CHOOSING JOY AS WE FORGIVE

Elizabeth Morris is a living example of the power of forgiveness. Several years ago just before Christmas, she received a phone call from the hospital. Her eighteen-year-old son Ted had been killed in a head-on collision. The driver of the other car received only minor lacerations. He had three times the legal limit of alcohol in his bloodstream. His name was Tommy.

Elizabeth and her husband Frank were devastated. The promise of their son's life had been destroyed in an instant by a drunk driver. Elizabeth and Frank went to the courtroom where the young man was arraigned on a charge of manslaughter. They were sickened to hear him plead, "Not guilty."

In her grief, Elizabeth wrestled with Christ's call to forgiveness. It seemed so horribly unfair that her own son should die and Tommy should live. "If I ever see him walking across the street," she once told her husband, "I'll run him down!"

Weeks dragged into months as Tommy's case went through postponement after postponement. The young man remained free, never having spent a night in jail, and he still carried a valid driver's license. Elizabeth's hatred intensified to a point where she could think and talk of nothing else but seeing Tommy punished. Finally the sentence was handed down: five years' probation. Elizabeth was outraged. The man who had killed her son would go free.

During this time, God was at work on Elizabeth's heart. She began to hear lines from the Bible playing in her mind:

"Forgive, not seven times, but seventy times seven…
Love your enemies….Do not take revenge."

She wrestled with conflicting impulses — the desire to forgive warred against the desire for revenge. The battle continued.

One day she sat in the auditorium of the high school where Ted had graduated. As part of his probation, Tommy was required to speak to the students at a special assembly organized by the group,

Mothers Against Drunk Driving. Elizabeth wanted to hear what Tommy had to say. "I want to tell you about the night I killed Ted Morris," he began, a look of anguish on his face. "I got drunk, I got in a car, and I killed a young man who was just about the same age as a lot of you kids. When they told me Ted had died, I couldn't stop crying. To think of all the people I hurt — the truth is, they should've put me in prison."

Elizabeth couldn't believe what she was hearing. All along she had pictured Tommy as a monster without a conscience. Now she saw him as a broken young man, drowning in guilt.

Over the coming weeks, Elizabeth made a point of getting to know this young man. Day by day, her feelings wavered between sympathy and revulsion. Sometimes she would smell alcohol on his breath, and the old hatred would revive. Yet, there was an air of sorrow and tragedy about Tommy that tugged at her heart.

"How much are you drinking?" she asked him one time.

"I start drinking every day after work. I put a pillow on the phone to keep it from ringing, and then I drink until I fall asleep."

Eventually, Tommy's drinking led him to break probation and he was forced to go to jail. When Elizabeth discovered he had no visitors, she went to see him. Sitting across from Tommy, she felt a wave of compassion come over her. It didn't make sense. *This is the man who killed Ted*, she kept telling herself. Yet, she could feel the last dregs of her hatred draining away. They talked for a while, and finally Tommy said, "Mrs. Morris, I'm so sorry about Ted. Would you, could you please forgive me?"

"I forgive you, Tommy," she replied. "But I want you to forgive me, too."

"Forgive you? For what?"

"I used to hate you."

In time, Elizabeth came to understand Tommy's troubled background and his desperate desire to break his alcohol addiction. She also remembered Jesus said not only to forgive your enemies, but to do good to them. So she began doing good to Tommy. She visited him, encouraged him in his recovery from alcoholism, and explained to him how Christ could give him a completely new life.

Tommy was sometimes released in the Morrises' custody so that they could take him to different schools where he gave talks to teenagers, or to the Morrises' church on Sundays. On one trip, they were driving near the church when Tommy said, "I was reading in my Bible that a Christian is supposed to be baptized. I think I'm ready." Because the Morrises' church allowed laypeople to baptize, they drove directly to the church and Frank took Tommy into the baptistery. It was the same church where Frank had performed the same ceremony for his then eleven-year-old son, Ted. As Elizabeth watched, Frank Morris baptized Tommy.

After Tommy was paroled, Elizabeth and Frank often invited him to their home. He hasn't had a drink since he left prison. Tommy likes to help Elizabeth and Frank, cutting their grass or doing other chores. When Tommy visits the Morrises', he feels like he's home. Elizabeth Morris and her husband Frank found inner peace in the midst of their grief through the powerful act of forgiveness.

Christ taught us to pray: "*Forgive us our debts, as we forgive our debtors.*" (Matthew 6:12) There is a growing wealth of psychological research demonstrating that when we authentically honor that prayer in our daily lives, a myriad of health benefits will touch our hearts.

Forgiveness is the act of consciously deciding, with the help of God, to let go of all the resentment, hatred or bitterness we have toward another person. It does not mean forgetting or condoning the wrongdoing committed against us.

Living with total forgiveness toward all who have harmed you or your loved ones enables a deeper sense of peace to come into your heart, builds up greater immunity for your ongoing health, protects you against ongoing stress, lowers your blood pressure — and some studies now indicate will even lengthen your life span.

I still remember Pope John Paul II going to a prison in Rome in January, 1984 to offer his forgiveness to Mehmet Ali Agca, the 26-year-old terrorist who had attempted to kill him two years earlier. This simple act of forgiveness sent shock waves through the world's news media, and prompted *Time* Magazine to devote a cover article under the simple title, *"Why Forgive?"* In that same issue, Time Senior Columnist, Lance Morrow wrote:

> *"Christ preached forgiveness, the loving of one's enemies. It is at the center of the New Testament. Forgiveness is not an impulse that is in much favor these days. The prevalent style in the world runs more to the hard, cold eye of the avenger. Forgiveness does not look much like a tool for survival in a bad world. But that is what it is."*

Over the years as I've visited with many people in the aftermath of mistreatment, I've discovered a perspective on forgiveness that is often helpful: *We may be better able to move beyond our mistreatment if we understand that our offender was, in fact, a broken person.* When we see that there may have been factors in the offender's life that lead him to be the way he is, our image of that offender changes. We experience an important perspective shift; we move from pure resentment toward that offender to compassionate understanding of that offender.

Perspective is a key to forgiveness. A perspective which seeks to understand rather than hate parallels the perspective of Jesus on the cross. *"Father, forgive them,* "he said, *"for they do not know what they are doing."* Jesus forgave his tormentors because he understood they didn't grasp the monstrous nature of their crime. That's a quantum leap in perspective.

When we experience that same quantum transformation in our perspective, then we can say, "Father, forgive that abusive stepparent, or that manipulative friend, or that unfaithful spouse, or that rebellious child — because, Father, he just doesn't know what he's doing. I realize now he's had so much brokenness in his own life that it's no wonder he treats people this way."

Jesus' perspective on forgiveness is one which can carry us through every unfair trial we face in this life, even a trial which leads to death itself. One person who exemplified this Christ-like perspective in the very moment of death was Edith Louisa Cavell, an English nurse who served with the Red Cross at the turn of the century. As director of the nursing staff at the Berkendael Medical Institute in Brussels, she helped to greatly improve the status and standards of nursing around the world. During World War I, when Belgium was overrun by the German army, she voluntarily remained at the Berkendael Institute and supervised its conversion into a Red Cross hospital. She also joined an underground movement which helped British, French, and Belgian solders escape to the Netherlands, a neutral country.

In August 1915, Edith Cavell was arrested by the Germans, along with a Belgian member of the underground, Phillippe Baucq. By this time, she and Baucq had helped more than two hundred men escape to safety. Two months after their arrest, Cavell and Baucq were tried and sentenced to death. On October 11, they were lead before a firing squad. As the German soldiers bound her to a post and blindfolded her, Edith turned to her condemned friend and said, "It is not enough to die for our countries. We must have no hatred or bitterness toward the Germans." Moments later, she and Phillippe Baucq were dead.

Edith Cavell understood something about forgiveness that we, too, must understand. The goal of forgiveness is not just reconciliation. Nor is the final goal of forgiveness just emotional healing. Ultimately, we forgive others because God has forgiven us. *"Bear with each other,"* writes Paul in Colossians 3:13, *"and forgive whatever grievances you may have against one another. Forgive as the Lord forgave you."* The more completely we forgive, the more completely we identify with Christ. Our goal as Christians is to become more and more like Christ, and one way we do that is by forgiving like Christ. As we choose this courageous path, we discover that a wonderful by-product of that decision is that we are also choosing joy.

Chapter 6
CHOOSING JOY THROUGH HEALTHY AGING

Whatever you do, do it with all your heart, as though you were doing it unto the Lord, and not for men."

Colossians 3:23

During the past 20 years, I have read over 100 books that seek to address the various components that characterize healthy aging. These authors, psychologists, theologians, sociologists, physicians, nutritional scientists, exercise physiologists, gerontologists and research technologists seem to converge in affirming seven crucial characteristics of heathy aging.

As I share my personal pilgrimage regarding these seven attributes, I realize you may have come to different conclusions than my own. I do hope whatever our personal convictions about healthy aging may be, that we will all regularly evaluate ourselves in these seven areas as an act of love for our families, friends and for all who care about us and our well-being.

Let's look together at what I call *The Seven Pillars of Joyful Aging* because whether we are age 30 or age 90, these seven characteristics are crucial for our spiritual, emotional, mental and physical health.

1. A Vital Spiritual Life

One characteristic that I often communicate to my children that they should always expect of me as their father is that I am growing spiritually. For me, this begins each morning with a quiet time of prayer before the sun rises. Utilizing scripture and a prayer list with the names of loved ones who have requested prayer, I spend a season in prayer and meditation. I end the prayer with the request that my life might be marked today by a sweet aroma of compassion and unconditional love shared with all people and animals. I then do some deep breathing while inhaling the word "gratitude" and exhaling the word "kindness", praying these words will guide my life today.

Other components of a vital spiritual life often include:

- Fellowship with other Christians
- Bible study
- Living in loving accountable relationships with Christian friends
- Proactively caring for the marginalized of our society *("the least of these"* Matthew 25:40)
- Consistent worship and service in our churches
- Sharing the good news of our liberating master

2. A Strong Social Network

Sociologists and gerontologists coincide in their research affirming the essential need of a strong and vital social network for any of us who would seek to age in a healthy fashion.

Dan Buettner, in his groundbreaking book, *The Blue Zones: Lessons for Living Longer from People Who've Lived the Longest,* strongly verifies the reality that in the five communities in the world with the longest living men and women (Sardinia, Italy; Okinawa, Japan; Loma Linda, California; the Nicoya Peninsula of Costa Rica; and Ikaria, Greece), a pivotal characteristic is a passionate commitment to family and to developing deep friendships. Research clearly indicates that a dangerous tendency of many aging people is a gradual movement toward isolation. It is hard to overstate the damage social isolation can do to our health and potential longevity. One recent meta-analysis initiated by the U.S. Council on Aging concluded: *"Social isolation and loneliness are associated with increased mortality. Social isolation has also been linked to other adverse health effects, including dementia and increased risk for hospital admission from all causes."*

One meta-study researching healthy men and women over the age of 100 concludes: *"Perhaps the most common factor among known centenarians is the presence of strong social bonds, deeply rooted relationships and/or some form of active engagement that provides a passion for facing each day anew. This cannot be overstated."*

3. Cognitive Challenge

Research clearly indicates that every brain changes with age, and mental function changes along with it. Mental decline is a common and feared consequence of aging. However, cognitive decline is not inevitable with aging. In order to reverse decline, we must commit to daily cognitive challenge.

Significant scientific research has clearly indicated that we can stimulate new connections between nerve cells and even generate new cells through a process called "neuroplasticity". Any mentally stimulating activity can help to build your cognitive reserve. Here are some examples:

- Take classes in academic disciplines you have not studied before
- Block out at least one hour a day to read material that stretches you mentally
- Learn a foreign language
- Decide to take music lessons on a new instrument
- Learn a new computer program
- Memorize scripture verses
- Teach a class in your church or in your community
- Mentor a young person who wants to learn more in his or her field of interest
- Join a book club that is studying challenging books. Research indicates that people who participate in classes and other social activities that include homework reading were 40% less

likely to develop memory loss than those who chose not to participate in these activities.

Scientific research is verifying words that Henry Ford wrote years ago: *"Anyone who stops learning is old, whether at twenty or eighty. Anyone who keeps learning stays young."*

4. Meaningful Acts of Service to Others

German physician, theologian and missionary to the poorest of poor in Africa, Albert Schweitzer wrote wisely when he stated, *"I don't know what your destiny will be, but one thing I know: the only among you who will be truly happy are those who sought and found how to serve."* Having worked with men for over five decades, I've watched the painful transition of many who retired from meaningful work, and then felt a deep sense of confusion and depression as they struggled to fill their days.

Whatever our age, it is of crucial importance to us to understand that God created us in such a way that we can find joyful meaning and purpose as we live a life of service to others.

In the five communities where people live the longest in vibrant health, the word "retirement" is never found in their vocabularies. Research indicates that actively serving others is not only good for our bodies as we age, but also offers many benefits to our emotional well-being. According to a study conducted by the Corporation for National & Community Service, 67% of "retired" men and women reported that while they often sensed a lack of companionship before volunteering in some way to serve others — they were now experiencing an increasing meaning, joy and purpose in their lives by serving.

I have been particularly intrigued by the growing myriad of studies of the life-style patterns of centenarians. Many of these studies reveal that aside from taking excellent care of their physical health, these folks seem to share the common characteristic of enjoying serving and engaging with other loved ones. Once again, this research clearly indicated that people who lived in isolation, not contributing to the lives of others, did not thrive.

Dr. Walter M. Bortz, an 88-year old clinical professor of medicine at Stanford University, suggests from his research that living a life of active service may lower the risk of dementia by reducing both stress and cardiovascular disease risk factors that are also associated with brain diseases. Dr. Bortz called this phenomenon "the necessity of being necessary." After Jesus washed his disciples' feet on the night before his crucifixion, he stated, *"I have done this for you as an example."* (John 13:15) and in so doing called all of us to a life of service and ministry to others.

What we are discovering in this generation of scientific research is that when we honor our Lord's command to serve, we enhance our own potential for a long and healthy life.

5. Consistent Exercise

Dan Buettner in his book *The Blue Zone Solution* verifies that research into the lifestyles of the citizens of the five communities with the longest-living population all shared one primary characteristic. They all moved naturally throughout the day. Dr. Buettner writes:

> *"The world's longest living people don't necessarily pump iron, run marathons or join gyms. Instead, they live in environments that constantly nudge them into moving. They grow gardens and don't have mechanical conveniences for house and yard work. Every trip to work, to a friend's house, or to church services occasions a walk."*

If we are physically able to do so, simply choosing to walk every day throughout the day is a wonderful commitment to make as we pursue a life of consistent exercise. If you have access to a smart phone, you may want to use a free app like "Steps", which records the number of steps you take daily. Many exercise physiologists and gerontologists suggest averaging at least 10,000 steps per day (approximately 5 miles). I've found that a goal of 12,000 – 14,000 steps encourages me to leave home and walk in God's creation or at the gym at least 2-3 times per day.

In addition to walking, some type of cardiovascular exercise, where you significantly increase your heart rate for approximately 30 minutes several times a week, is beneficial. (You can google "VO2 max" to discover what the maximum range of heart beats per minute should be when choosing aerobic exercise.)

As you probably know, the list of advantages of consistent cardio (aerobic) exercise is long and very compelling. The benefits include:

- Improving heart function
- Strengthening muscles
- Improving blood pressure
- Increasing HDL cholesterol (the "good" cholesterol in your blood)
- Improving blood flow to the brain which is significant for cognitive memory
- Improving mood in people who battle depression
- Lowering triglyceride levels
- Assisting in weight control
- Reducing cancer risk
- Reducing the incidence of stroke
- For many, increasing inner peace, a sense of well-being and stress reduction
- Significantly increases most individual's feelings of self-efficacy

It is difficult to overemphasize a comprehensive exercise program of cardio, stretching and weight training for those who seek to age in a healthy fashion. Dr. James Fries from the Standford Medical

Center, after a 20-year massive research project comparing men and women ages 59 through 79, summarized his conclusions: *"The study has a very strong exercise message. If you had to pick one thing to make people healthier, it would be aerobic exercise. The health benefits are far greater than we thought."*

One covenant I made years ago that you may want to consider addresses 3 of the 7 "pillars". I covenant to spend at least:

1. One hour a day in exercise
2. One hour a day in reading challenging materials
3. One hour a day with a family member or friend

6. Excellent Nutrition

A growing body of research clearly indicates that the cornerstone of most centenarian diets includes fruits, vegetables, seeds, lentils, healthy fats (avocados, walnuts, flax seeds, almonds, chia seeds, etc.), and plant based proteins (chickpeas, quinoa, beans, peanuts, etc.)

I have been deeply influenced by the meticulous research of Dr. Dean Ornish, Dr. Joel Fuhrman, Dr. Neal Barnard, Dr. Caldwell Esselstyn, Dr. Michael Greger, Dr. T. Colin Campbell, Dr. Garth Davis, and Dr. John McDougall — all of whom encourage us to move toward a whole food, plant based diet. Dr. Fuhrman, in his best-selling book *Eat to Live,* summarized his thirty years of research into a practical, daily acronym which I've sought to follow for many years: G-BOMBS.

The letters of the acronym stand for: Greens, Berries, Onions, Mushrooms, Beans and Seeds (including nuts). Further, Dr. Fuhrman writes wisely when he states, *"The most important thing to remember about food labels is that you should avoid foods that have labels."* If you have not already done so, to move away from all processed foods would be a wonderful first step you could take today as you move toward a whole food plant based diet."

As you are probably aware, there is a vast body of growing research warning us about the link between meat and disease. For example, researchers from the National Cancer Institute conducted a 16-year study which concluded that regular consumption of meat increases the risk of nine major diseases, including cancer, type 2 diabetes, stroke, Alzheimer's and heart disease. Multiple studies such as this one offer us even more motivation to move toward a whole food plant based diet. By way of personal witness, I have lived for many years following a strict whole food plant based, very low sugar, vegan diet and have experienced greater energy, increased running speed, stronger blood panel markers, and improved overall health.

7. Restorative Sleep

As you probably know, recent research clearly indicates the crucial need for deep, restorative sleep. Sleep plays a vital part in healthy aging in a number of ways. For example, sleep helps protect us from an increased risk of heart disease, kidney disease, high blood pressure, type two diabetes, high blood sugar levels, and stroke. In the past five years, breakthrough meta-studies also indicate the pivotal role of sleep in brain health. Deep, restorative sleep plays a housekeeping role that removes toxins in our brains that build up while we are awake. It has been clearly demonstrated that chronic insomnia increases the risk of various types of dementia.

Many years ago, my desire to improve my sleep quality led me to participate in a 3-month program sponsored by The Stanford Center for Sleep Disorders. Practical guidance from physicians at Stanford and other research included the following suggestions:

- Consider a 10 to 12 hour "technology fast" with all technological devices (computer, smartphones, television, etc.), turned off and ideally out of your bedroom every evening.
- Make certain your bedroom is quiet, dark, and cool.

- Develop a consistent spiritual disciple of prayer at bedtime, surrendering your life and your rest to God.
- Reduce blue light exposure throughout the entire evening.
- Begin each day with bright light exposure, ideally with a walk or run in nature.
- Consume no caffeine after lunch time.
- Develop a ritual of going to bed at the same time every night, including weekends.
- If needed, consider a melatonin supplement (Melatonin is a key sleep hormone that relaxes our brains).
- Limit or abstain from alcohol (alcohol in the evening alters melatonin production and decreases the natural nighttime elevation in human growth hormone (HGH) which plays a key role in circadian rhythms).
- Refrain from eating late in the evening.
- Exercise regularly, ideally in the morning. Multiple studies link vigorous exercise with improved sleep.

II Corinthians 10:31 has long guided me as I seek to live my life by the Seven Pillars of Joyfully Aging. It reads simply, but profoundly:

"So, whether you eat or drink, or whatever you do, do all in the glory of God."

Chapter 7

CHOOSING JOY BY OVERCOMING ANXIETY

Several years ago, my daughter Rachael emailed me the following touching story written by Ann Wells. It reads as follows:

My brother-in-law opened the bottom drawer of my sister's bureau and lifted out a tissue-wrapped package.

"This," he said, "is not a slip. This is lingerie." He discarded the tissue and handed me the slip. It was exquisite: silk, handmade and trimmed with a cobweb of lace. The price tag was still attached.

"Jan bought this the first time she went to New York, at least eight or nine years ago. She never wore it. She was saving it for a special occasion. Well, I guess this is the occasion." He took the slip from me and put it on the bed with the other clothes we were taking to the mortician.

His hands lingered on the soft material for a moment, then he slammed the drawer shut and turned to me. "Don't ever save anything for a special occasion. Every day you're alive is a special occasion."

I remembered those words through the funeral and the days that followed when I helped him and my niece attend to all the sad chores that follow an unexpected death. I thought about them on the plane returning to California from the Midwestern town where my sister's family lives.

I'm still thinking about his words, and they've changed my life. I'm reading more and dusting less. I'm sitting on the deck and admiring the view without fussing about the weeds in the garden. I'm spending more time with my family and friends and less time in committee meetings. I'm not 'saving' anything now; we

*use our good china and crystal for every special event
such as losing a pound, getting the sink unstopped, the
first rose blossom.*

*The terms "someday" and "one of these days" are
losing their grip on my vocabulary. If it's worth seeing or hearing or doing, I want to see and hear and do
it now. It's all those things left undone that would
make me angry if I knew that my hours were limited.*

*Angry because I put off seeing good friends whom
I was going to get in touch with someday. Angry because I hadn't written certain letters that I intended to
write one of these days. Angry and sorry that I didn't
tell my husband and daughter often enough how much
I truly love them. I'm trying very hard not to put off,
hold back or save anything that would add laughter
and luster to our lives. And every morning when I
open my eyes, I tell myself that every day, every minute, every breath truly is...a gift from God.*

Ann Wells, reflecting on how she is joyfully learning to live a
more serene and less anxious life.

The Apostle Paul addresses our tendency to live life with anxiety
by writing in Philippians 4:6 *"Do not worry about anything, but in
everything by prayer and supplication with thanksgiving, let your
requests be made known to God."* An excellent paraphrase of one
section of this verse reads simply, *"Worry about nothing, pray about
everything."* Then the Apostle Paul immediately leads us further by
giving us three guidelines to apply to our daily lives *in place of* living
a life of fear.

1. Live Life Joyfully

In the flow of the Greek text, Paul in Philippians 4:4 gives us a command that we are to live life joyfully. In Proverbs 17:22, we read, *"A joyful heart is good medicine."* Literally in the Hebrew text, this Scripture reads: *"A joyful heart of laughter brings healing."*

Norman Cousins in his books, *An Anatomy of An Illness* and *The Healing Heart*, and Dr. Dean Ornish in his books *Stress, Diet and Your Heart*, and *Love and Survival* clearly demonstrate the therapeutic value for our health when we trade in anxiety for joy.

For many years, I have believed that we are to love people into the Kingdom, and that our unconditional love will touch the heart of the non-Christian — and that God's Spirit will use that love to win the non-Christian to faith in Jesus Christ. I believe that more than ever today as I have seen God's faithfulness again and again.

But, I have also come to believe in more recent years that there are many non-Christians who may not be easily touched by the love we extend, but who will be deeply moved by a life marked by joy and peace, even in the midst of life's trials and heartaches.

Have you ever noticed that the first three "Fruit of the Spirit" are Love, Joy and Peace? I have often observed that there are those friends among us who may not be touched by our love, but they will observe:

- A Christian couple who have a son with cerebral palsy
- A Christian who is battling an unexpected financial crisis
- A Christian who is battling a serious illness
- A Christian family who cares for a frail, feeble, weakened parent day and night

And the manner in which these Christians radiate joy in the midst of their challenges impacts their non-Christian friends, and the Spirit of God often leads those loved ones to Christ because of these beautiful lives. Love, Joy, Peace!

Paul offers a second guideline as we seek to overcome anxiety:

2. Learn to Authentically Relax

In Philippians 4:5, we read, *"Let your forbearance be known by all people."* The Greek term we weakly translate as "forbearance" literally means "relaxation". *"Let your relaxation be known by all people."* My hunch is that in many congregations there will *never* be a message preached from the pulpit encouraging the members to learn to relax. We are wise to remember that Jesus had to remind his Type A driven disciples, *"Come apart and rest awhile."* (Mark 6:31)

In Philippians 4:11, Paul tells us that he had to *learn* to be content through the peaks and valleys of life. Contentment didn't come naturally to him. As he surrendered his whole life to Christ, he grew in his understanding of how to live with relaxation and contentment in his life, no matter the outward circumstances. So must we!

3. Take Time to Rest

Paul's third guideline for us as we wrestle with anxiety is to be certain we take time to rest. *"And the shalom* (could be translated 'rest') *of God which surpasses all comprehension will keep your hearts and minds in Christ Jesus."* (Philippians 4:7)

One practical way I have sought to honor this third guideline is to take a Sabbath Day once a week. For me, this day is filled with a more developed time of prayer and meditation, a long hike or jog in nature, spiritual readings, and relational time with family.

Wayne Muller writes wisely when he states,

"Sabbath is more than the absence of work; it is not just a day off when we catch up on television or errands. It is the presence of something that arises when we consecrate a period of time to listen to what is most deeply beautiful, nourishing, or true. It is time sanctified with our attention, our mindfulness, honoring those quiet forces of grace that sustain and heal us. Like a path

through the forest, Sabbath creates a marker for ourselves
so, if we are lost, we can find our way back to God."

A great privilege for me during my six-year ministry with the Minnesota Vikings was to speak at chapel services not only for the Vikings players, but also for the opposing teams that had traveled to Minneapolis. A faithful attendee at chapels held for the Chicago Bears was Walter Payton, one of the greatest running backs in the history of the N.F.L.

When Walter was diagnosed with a rare form of liver disease, his inner peace in the midst of this illness that would take his life at the age of 45 impacted many for Christ. Coach Mike Ditka often stated, *"Walter Payton was the greatest football player I ever saw, but he was an even greater person."* Walter wasn't always that way, but Christ transformed his life and gave him a peace that surpassed human comprehension. He died at rest, content.

Three guidelines from Philippians 4:4 aid us as we discover *The Anxiety Cure*. A simple way to remember them as we seek to put them in practice this week would be:

Rejoice (Philippians 4:4)
Relax (Philippians 4:5)
Rest (Philippians 4:7)

The Apostle Paul now gives us three Spiritual Disciplines as he continues in Philippians 4:4:

The First Spiritual Discipline: Feed Your Mind with Positive Thoughts

The Power of Positive Thinking wasn't an idea originated by pastor and author Norman Vincent Peale in his best-selling book in 1952. It is an idea that was originated by God, given to the Apostle Paul in Philippians 4. In verse 8 of this chapter Paul writes, *"Whatever is true, whatever is honorable, whatever is just, whatever is pure, whatever is lovely, whatever is gracious… think about these things."*

Paul is addressing the crucial issue of attitude. Some of us are facing difficult circumstances these days, and we realize we can't always control the outer situations of life, but we can control —with the help of God — our response to them. I've come to deeply believe that one of the most important God-empowered skills we can develop as Christians is to learn *to reframe our thinking.*

A central component to truly discover *The Anxiety Cure* can be found in an acronym developed by Dr. Martin Seligman, the pioneer of positive psychology. The Acronym: *ABC*

A = Adversity
B = Beliefs
C = Consequences

For example, an adversity enters our lives like an unwelcomed guest. This trial could range from a bad cold to an unwanted divorce to pancreatic cancer. Adversity.

Our beliefs about this adversity are the pivotal key! Do our beliefs center in what we know about God's love for us? Here a crucial question always is: Where is my gaze, and where is my glance? Is my gaze upon God, and my glance at the unwanted circumstance? Or, is my gaze on the trial with just a passing glance toward God and His love for me? Beliefs.

This leads to consequences. Our beliefs will either lead us into depression and anxiety, or, our beliefs will lead us to the consequence of becoming more conformed into the image of Christ, which is our goal. Adversity. Beliefs. Consequences.

Feed your mind with positive thoughts.

The Second Spiritual Discipline: Focus Your Attention Toward Worthy Models

In Philippians 4:9, Paul writes, *"What you have learned and re-*

ceived and heard and seen in me put into practice." Throughout scripture, we are encouraged to focus our attention on worthy models. Reflect with me: Do we have two or three worthy models, mature Christians who are consistently building the character of their lives in Christ into us?

Furthermore, this second Spiritual Discipline is one reason I believe Christians need to commit themselves to the reading of quality Christian biographies. How many of us have ever read a biography on the life of Dietrich Bonhoeffer, Mother Teresa, Henri Nouwen, Corrie ten Boom, William Booth, C.S. Lewis, William Carey, Jim Elliott, Hudson Taylor, Billy Graham?

What if some of us choose to trade in another mystery or romance novel for a moving biography about a man or woman used in a powerful way by God?

Focus your attention on worthy models.

The Third Spiritual Discipline: Discover God's Peace in Every Circumstance

When the Apostle Paul writes in Philippians 4:11-12 that he has learned to be content in every circumstance, whether in plenty or want, well-fed or hungry, he calls us to come to a point in our walk with Christ where we can say from our hearts:

> *"Whether I'm in a comfortable home or a hut in India, married or unmarried, healthy or battling illness, underneath it all I've learned in whatever circumstance to be content because I know who I am in Christ."*

- Feed your mind with positive thoughts.
- Focus your attention toward worthy models.
- Discover God's peace in every circumstance.

When we honor these three Spiritual Disciplines, and begin to build them into the fabric of our lives, then with authenticity we can say that marvelous affirmation from Philippians 4:13, *"I can do all things through Christ who strengthens me."*

Years ago, there was a little girl named "Norma" who desperately needed to know the reality of the love of Christ. Norma was born out of wedlock, and she lived the early years of her life being frequently abused, physically, sexually, psychologically. She was raped at the tender age of eight. Her mother experienced an emotional breakdown. Norma never knew her father.

Norma's anxiety intensified as she lived in foster home after foster home, twelve in all. Then she moved to an orphanage. She once wrote, *"What was so difficult about my childhood was that there was never a constant model of unconditional love. There was never a person I knew would be there tomorrow."*

In her adolescent years, Norma was told by some self-serving men that they would take her to Hollywood and make her a star. In a desperate attempt to find unconditional love, she lived a very broken life, went through a series of affairs, and two failed marriages. One morning, Norma was found dead of an apparent overdoes of drugs which were lying next to her bed, and with the phone dangling off its hook, perhaps suggesting that in the middle of the night, she was struggling to find someone to reach out to, who would truly love her. And knowing no one, in an act of great brokenness, she took her life.

Years later, Elton John recorded a song about her life. You may remember the lyrics of the refrain: *"And it seemed to me you lived your life like a candle in the wind never knowing who to cling to when the rain set in."*

The song was written about Norma Jean Baker, better known by her stage name, Marilyn Monroe.

In whatever community we live in, there are scores of Norma Jean Bakers. They live their lives like a candle in the wind, never knowing who to cling to when the rains of life set in.

The good news of Philippians 4 is that we can cling to Christ! And we can help the Normas of our little cities to cling to Him, too, as together we discover *The Anxiety Cure* and experience God's rest and peace and joy.

Chapter 8

CHOOSING JOY AS WE EXPERIENCE HEALING FROM MISTREATMENT

Karl and Edith Taylor had been married for twenty-three years. Edith considered herself "the luckiest woman on the block" to be married to such a loving, thoughtful man. In his job with the government, Karl often had to go out of town, but he always wrote her faithfully, and sent her a gift from every place he visited.

When Karl learned he was being assigned to Okinawa for a few months, the Taylors were saddened. It would be a long separation, but to keep their spirits up they made plans to put a down payment on a cozy little cottage just as soon as Karl returned.

So Karl went to Okinawa, and Edith was thrilled when his thoughtful cards and letters began to arrive. There were no gifts this time, but Edith knew her husband was putting every spare cent into savings for their dream house. Within a few weeks, however, the letters became fewer and briefer. Edith received word from Karl that he would have to stay three more weeks. Later, he wrote, "just one more month." Then, "a couple of months longer."

Finally, after Karl had been gone over a year, Edith received the letter that shattered her heart. It began, "Dear Edith, I wish there were a kinder way to tell you we are no longer married…" Karl had obtained a mail-order divorce from Mexico, and he was now married to a nineteen-year-old Japanese girl named "Aiko".

Edith was devastated. The world ceased to make sense to her. There was no sound, no color, no taste anymore — only unrelieved pain. Finally, Edith took all her anguished feelings and honestly spread them out before God in prayer. As she wrestled with God, she realized she had a choice to make: she could become bitter and resentful, hating Karl for his betrayal and mistreatment of her — or she could choose to continue to love him. After a deep inner struggle, Edith made the healing choice for her trial of mistreatment: she wrote to Karl, told him she forgave him, and asked that they continue to keep in touch.

So, for the next few years Karl and Edith exchanged cards and letters frequently. As time went by, Karl wrote Edith to tell her of his and Aiko's first child, a girl named "Marie"; then two years later another little girl named "Helen".

A couple more years went by, and Edith received another letter that broke her heart: Karl was dying of lung cancer. The medical bills were mounting, taking all the money Karl had saved to send his two little girls to school in America. Aiko and the girls would soon be left without anyone to provide for them. "What's going to happen to them now?" was the closing, despairing question of one of his letters.

Edith wrote back that she would like to pay the airfares to bring Marie and Helen to the states to live with her, if Karl and Aiko agreed. So a short time after Karl's death, fifty-four-year-old Edith Taylor became "the other mother" to a three-year-old and a five-year-old. A few months later, Edith arranged for Aiko to join her and the girls in America.

At the airport, Edith waited until the last person came off the plane — a frail Japanese woman who seemed totally alone and afraid. Edith called Aiko's name, and they rushed into each other's arms. There they promised that together they would raise the girls for Christ. Edith Taylor later wrote, "Though Karl was taken from me, God has given me three others to love." She offered her trial of mistreatment to God, and God *transformed* her trial into healing for Aiko, Marie and Helen — and for Edith herself. That's what God wants to do in our lives when we are victims of mistreatment.

Years ago, I participated in a pastors' conference in Seoul, Korea. There I met a remarkable man, Dr. Kim Joon-Gon. Dr. Kim survived the Communist persecution of the church during the Korean War, and was one of the leading spokesmen for the amazing revival that swept Korea. As we were having breakfast together one morning, he told me his story.

During the Korean War, Dr. Kim was in a Communist-controlled area for three months. One night, he was held by soldiers, and forced to watch while his wife and parents were tortured and murdered by one Communist official. He, himself was then beaten, and left unconscious. He revived during the night, located his baby daughter — the only remaining member of his family — and escaped.

He was recaptured by the Communists, and beaten again. Starving and suffering from massive injuries, Dr. Kim again faced the cruelty of the same Communist official who had murdered his family. During that time he went in and out of consciousness. He was so exhausted and defeated that he had ceased praying; he had lost all hope that God would answer. He was in total despair, a spiritual condition which he described to me as "the darkness of spiritual death, complete separation from God."

But even in his darkness, God was working in Dr. Kim's life. There came a moment in his suffering and hopelessness when he suddenly awoke to the realization that his lips were moving — and the words he spoke were words of prayer. "God was speaking to me and through me," Dr. Kim said. "In that moment I had gone from death to life. I felt joy and peace spring up in my heart. Our loving God had brought me through the valley of the shadow of death — and He was calling me to go and talk to the hated man who had murdered my family."

So Dr. Kim began to pray for his Communist persecutor — and as he prayed, he found new strength, new freedom, new life. Then he rose and went to this man and told him that he loved him, and that God loved him, too. This Communist was startled at first to see that Dr. Kim was even alive, but he was absolutely thunderstruck when he heard this ragged, battered, half-dead prisoner begin to talk about the forgiveness offered through Christ.

"This Communist leader could not believe I would come to him in love," Dr. Kim concluded. "He began to weep over his sins, and over the killing of my family. He committed himself to Christ, and became a completely changed man from that day forward. Today that man is an elder in a church here in Korea, and he and I pray for each other every day."

Our trial of mistreatment can be a destructive force in our lives — or it can be an opportunity. The choice is ours to make. When we are mistreated, we can seize the opportunity to demonstrate to others that Christ is alive in us, even in times of trial. Our lives can become a joyful witness for Christ when we choose to respond in a supernatural, Christ-controlled way to the unfair treatment of others.

Chapter 9

CHOOSING JOY AS WE DEMONSTRATE AFFECTION TO OUR LOVED ONES

Miss Brown was a negative and critical woman without any living family members. Many years ago, a little boy named Teddy entered Miss Brown's fifth grade class as a lonely child transferred from a school in another town.

To Miss Brown, Teddy seemed marked for failure. In fact, whenever Teddy performed poorly on a test, Miss Brown would mark his paper with an extra-large "F", as if she derived some sort of perverse satisfaction from singling him out as a failure. Miss Brown hadn't bothered to check Teddy's school records, but if she had, she would have noticed the following notations:

> *First grade* — "Teddy shows promise, but he comes from a difficult home situation."
> *Second grade* — "Teddy is a good boy, but too serious. His mother is terminally ill."
> *Third grade* — "Teddy cooperates, but he is detached. His mother died this year."
> *Fourth grade*— "Teddy is a slow learner. His father shows no interest in him."

Clearly, there were reasons for Teddy's gradual slide toward failure that Miss Brown had never tried to understand.

At Christmas time, the boys and girls brought presents for their teacher. They sat in a circle and, one by one, Miss Brown opened her presents. At last she came to the present Teddy brought, and unwrapped it. She found a tarnished bracelet from which half the cut-glass stones were missing. Next to it was a half-empty bottle of cheap perfume. When the other children saw these second-hand gifts, they began to laugh.

For the first time since Teddy had come into her class, Miss Brown suddenly felt a twinge of pity for the boy. She immediately wrapped the battered bracelet on her wrist and dabbed some of the cheap perfume on her neck and wrists. After class, when all the other children had gone home, Teddy came to Miss Brown and said, "Miss Brown, you smell just like my mother used to before she died." And then, he affectionately hugged her.

That night, Miss Brown knelt beside her bed, and begged God to forgive her for her bitter and unloving spirit towards Teddy. That was the beginning of a new relationship between Miss Brown and Teddy. From that day forward, she never failed to seek out and develop Teddy's true worth and abilities. This was the beginning of Teddy's transformation.

Over the years that followed, Teddy kept in touch with Miss Brown, sending her an occasional note. One read, in part:

"Dear Miss Brown, I wanted you to be the first to know. Next week I'll be graduating second in my high school class. Love, Teddy"

A few years later, Teddy wrote:

"Dear Miss Brown: Just wanted to let you know I'll be graduating first in my class at the University. It was the hardest thing I've ever done, but it's also been the greatest experience of my life. Love, Teddy"

Then this, several years later:

"Dear Miss Brown, I made it! As of today, I am Theodore J. Simmons, M.D. How about that? And one more thing: I'm going to be married on July 27th, and I would be honored if you would come and sit where my mother would have sat.

My Dad died last year, and you're the only family I have now.

Love, Teddy"

Miss Brown went to Teddy's wedding and sat in the place of his mother. Today, Teddy is like a son to her, and his family is now her family.

Two lonely people — a middle-aged teacher and an isolated little boy — brought together through the power of *affection*.

Affection. People of all ages need affection. Years ago, when I was serving as a pastor, there was a 93-year old woman in our congregation. She was a widow and lived alone. She had no living family members. I used to hug her on Sunday morning when I would see her after worship, and on occasion, she would say to me, *"You know, when you hug me in our church hallway, that's the only time anyone ever touches me in my life. It means so much to me."*

Elderly people need the touch of love. So do little infants.

For twenty years, I travelled overseas once a year to speak, and seek to encourage mission workers. On several occasions, I was involved in hunger relief work in famine stricken countries. Feeding and holding malnourished babies, I was often reminded of words I had read years ago by Edmund Janss:

> *"In Madras, India, I once watched a house mother tenderly holding a baby. She was feeding her while humming a gentle song. The baby had been found in a trash heap softly crying. I asked the house mother about her feeding method. She nodded and said, 'If we don't hold them and stroke them, and touch them as we feed them, the babies die. But if we hold them and stroke them and touch them as we feed them, they generally live."*

There is an absolute necessity in all our lives of demonstrating affection.

The Apostle Paul affirms this reality throughout his letters. For example, in Romans 12:10, Paul writes, *"Love one another with brotherly affection."* The word we translate as "brotherly" into English in this verse conveys the idea of a "family-like affection." So what Paul is literally saying here is: *"I want you to strive to be affectionately devoted to all your Christian friends as if they were your parents, your siblings, your children."*

Later in Romans, Paul writes, *"Greet one another with a holy kiss."* (Romans 16:16)

One Christian mentor and friend who used to always greet me with a holy kiss was Ray Stedman, senior pastor of the Peninsula Bible Church and prolific author. Ray graduated into Eternity a number of years ago. Throughout the years, whenever we were reunited, we would always embrace, and Ray would kiss me on the neck with a holy kiss. Ray was such a wonderful mentor to me not only because of his wisdom and discernment as a Bible expositor, but also because he modeled so lovingly the demonstration of affection.

Many of the Christians I've met in Third World countries have risked their lives for the cause of Christ. Many have served time in prison for their faith. So often when I would prepare to leave these friends and fly back to the United States, they would hug me and kiss me on the left and right side of the neck and say, "We will always love you." It's been my observation that when you've been literally threatened with your life for the crime of loving Christ, there develops a very deep bond with your fellow believers, and that bond is often modeled through the godly demonstration of affection. Indeed, research indicates that there is reluctance in our culture, which is often not found in other cultures, to demonstrate affection — man to man, father to son, mother to daughter, Christian to Christian.

For example, Christian psychologists teach us that the most obvious way to convey unconditional love to a child is through appropriate physical contact. Yet studies indicate that many fathers are reluctant to show physical affection to their children, especially their sons.

Research indicates that girl infants receive five times as much physical affection than boy infants. Many psychologists believe this is a key component to the reality that six times as many young boys are referred to psychiatric clinics than girls in the United States.

An old friend of mine told me about a deeply moving experience immediately following the death of his father. My friend was quietly weeping in the hospital when a nurse came into the room and attempted to comfort him. My friend looked up at the nurse, and softly said, "You don't understand. I'm not crying because my dad died. Dad had been very sick for a long time, and was in a coma. It's a blessing he died. I'm not crying because he died. I'm crying because he died having never once hugged me, embraced me, or telling me that he loved me. I'm not crying because my father died. I'm crying because my father died, and I never really knew him."

The absolute importance of demonstrating affection

Consider with me the historical background surrounding Paul's admonition: *"Greet one another with a holy kiss"* (Romans 16:16). The 1st Century Assembly of the Christian Church at Rome was a gathering of a family of faith who was being purified through suffering. These Christians were being refined through persecution under the reign of Nero. Accordingly, the early church was forced to meet underground. These believers would meet each evening in a home for a meal and for deep fellowship and prayer. Often, if you were a 1st Century Christian and you were meeting in a home tonight, you would notice the gathering was a bit smaller than the night before. During the past 24 hours, one of your loved ones would have been arrested. The guards of Nero would have imprisoned or executed more followers of *The Way*. Early Christians lived with enormous uncertainty regarding their future.

After their meal together, the early Christians would set aside a portion of the bread and wine for the "Agape Love Feast", the celebration of Holy Communion. After the *Agape Love Feast*, it was time for the group of believers to disperse. But they didn't dare leave all at once, or some unfriendly observer might alert the authorities that secret meetings were taking place. So these Christians would slip from the house of the catacombs, one or two at a time. Before they left each other, they hugged, a powerful non-verbal expression of their mutual love. It was as if they were saying, *"I may never see you again in this life. But I want you to know I love you. I'll pray for you. If the soldiers come and take me to my death, I'll be waiting for you in eternity."*

Then, one last expression of their godly affection before parting: They would kiss each other on the left side of the neck, then on the right side. *A holy kiss.*

Years passed. Persecution waned. The underground church went above ground and became prosperous. The open demonstration of affection gradually declined. The "love feast" ceased to be a communal meal. It became an institutional service. Even though the sacrament of communion remains an important and overwhelmingly meaningful aspect of Christian worship, it is rarely practiced anymore with the kind of family-like intimacy it once entailed. The embrace that used to conclude first-century Christian worship disappeared. The holy kiss between believers was replaced by a kiss on the forehead by a priest as the believer received the sacrament of communion.

More time passed. The priest no longer kissed the believer's forehead during communion. Instead, he kissed the believer's hand. More time passed, and the kiss was removed from the believer altogether. Now the priest kissed an object rather than a person. He kissed the cup or a scroll containing some holy words or a stole, a band of cloth that the priest himself wore over his shoulders.

Do you see what has happened in the history of the church since the time of Paul? The affection God intended us to show one another in the body of Christ has gradually been transferred from people to things. This, in fact, is a parable of what has taken place in our lives. If we are honest, we have to confess that our own affection is all too easily transferred from people to such things as careers, homes, and financial investments.

In every home, in every congregation, in every community, there are men, women and children who are hurting, who are lonely, who are broken, who don't so much need our advice and counsel. They need the *touch of love*. They need the *demonstration of affection*. It needs to be done honorably. It needs to be done with integrity. It needs to be done in a holy way. It needs to be done in an appropriate way. *But, it needs to be done.*

As you may know, there is a medical phenomenon called "The Failure to Thrive Syndrome." Simply stated, the *Failure to Thrive Syndrome* teaches us that if you place an infant or a child battling an illness in a quality medical facility, but isolate that child from three human responses, the infant or child will become listless, sluggish, lethargic, critically ill and often die. What are the three human responses?

• *Eye contact*
• *Physical contact*
• *Focused attention*

Put another way, let's say you place two children under the exact same overall excellent medical care. But, with one child, you lavish him with loving eye contact, physical contact and compassionate focused attention. The second child you deprive of eye contact, physical contact and focused attention. The result is that the first child tends to thrive. The second child often dies. This is the *Failure to Thrive Syndrome.*

We must understand that what may take the life of an infant or child may also break the heart of an older loved one in our family or our circle of friends.

Many of the most joyful experiences of my life have come from simply demonstrating affection to the lonely, the forgotten elderly, abused children and animals, and to the brokenhearted. May we all be faithful in honoring our loving God through the joyful expression of affection.

Chapter 10

CHOOSING JOY IN THE MIDST OF LIFE'S GREATEST TRIALS

Perhaps like some of you, I grew up singing the Great Hymns of Faith. Whether it was around the piano in our church parsonage, or driving across Nebraska to Estes Park, Colorado for memorable vacations, our family used to spend hours together singing precious Gospel Hymns.

I cannot begin to tell you how many times in my own life during seasons of great trial or heartache that the lyrics of these anthems came back to my heart to comfort and sustain me. For me, after the Promises of Scripture and the love of family, it has been the tender words of beloved hymns that have brought peace and consolation in the midst of life's hard places.

There is a beautiful hymn written by F.W.H. Meyer which contains this verse:

> *"So through life and death, through sorrow or through sinning, Christ shall suffice me, for He hath sufficed. Christ is the end, for Christ is the beginning. Christ the beginning, for the end is Christ."*

Do you remember the lyrics of my mother's favorite hymn?
> *"When peace like a river attendeth my way, when sorrow like sea billows roll, whatever my lot, though hast taught me to say, 'It is well with my soul.'"*

Or have we ever deeply reflected on the reality of the words in the verse of that great hymn, *Trust & Obey:*

> *"Not a burden we bear, not a sorrow we share, but our toil He doth richly repay. Not a grief or a loss, not a frown nor a cross, but is blest if we trust and obey."*

My question for us is: How are these trials blest? How do we bring glory to God in the midst of life's greatest tragedies? What does He want us to understand in our hearts when struggles enter our lives like unwelcomed guests?

As we seek to answer these crucial questions, we discover that 1 Thessalonians will serve as a backdrop for four foundational principles that every Christian must build into his character in preparation for life's greatest storms.

As we turn to 1 Thessalonians, we discover that both the Apostle Paul and the Christians at Thessalonia were no strangers to the intruder of affliction. In 1 Thessalonians 3:2-3, Paul writes, *"we sent Timothy to you because we wanted to make certain you would not be unsettled by your trials."*

In 1 Thessalonians 3:4, Paul writes, *"When we were with you, you remember that we taught you to be prepared for trials."*

In 1 Thessalonians 3:7, Paul writes, *"In all our distress and trials, we have been comforted by your faith."*

Three times in five verses the word "trial" appears. This New Testament term literally means "pressure from circumstances". A good contemporary definition of this word would be: Anything in life that causes us to say to ourselves, "Oh no! Not this!" From an abrasive co-worker who ridicules us for our integrity all the way to the sudden news that a beloved family member has Stage Four Cancer — there are many degrees on the continuum of trials. Pressure from life's circumstances. "Oh no! Not this!"

One promise from Scripture we so often don't want to hear comes from the lips of our Lord, *"In this world, you will have tribulation."* (John 16:33).

- David writes, *"Many are the afflictions of the righteous."* (Psalm 34:19)

- Job acknowledged, *"Man's days are short lived and full of trouble."* (Job 14:1)

- Paul writes, *"We are knocked down... persecuted... perplexed."* (II Corinthians 4:9)

- Peter writes, *"Do not be surprised when various trials come into your life."* (1 Peter 4:12)

There is complete solidarity on this topic — the Bible is filled with verses and promises and illustrations and examples of the reality of the inevitability of trials.

As we wrestle with our response to life's greatest trials, I offer us four Biblical Principles that we can always hold in our hearts. These truths will serve us well in our hours of affliction and suffering:

1. The vast majority of trials that enter our lives can be at least partially understood if we grasp in our hearts and minds the biblical doctrine of free will.

Put another way, God in His Grace, has given us free will, and often we will rebel. When we do, this frequently brings both trials and heartaches to ourselves and to others.

A few years ago, I led a young man to Christ. He experienced God's grace and unconditional love in his heart and became a new man, living with integrity and compassion. We would meet together weekly and on occasion he would share about the life he had lived before surrendering his heart to Christ. It was a life of drug abuse, alcohol addiction, chain smoking and frequent all night parties. He had deeply hurt many people. While my friend experienced complete forgiveness from all his transgressions, he also fully understood that there would be consequences for his past choices as he exercised his free will. He died young as a direct result of his lifestyle of abuse and excess.

This is the hard reality of free will — not only in what we ingest into our bodies, but for all of the spiritual and relational choices we make — these decisions will often have painful consequences for ourselves and for those we love. We must understand that it is not really fair or therapeutic to take those choices that lead to deep heartache and lay those mistakes at the feet of God with blame and resentment. No, this category of trials is the result of our being given free will — and our subsequent willingness to rebel against a life of sacrificial love.

C.S. Lewis suggested that perhaps 90% of all suffering that will touch us and our loved ones in our lifetime could be at least partially understood if we would truly understand the biblical doctrine of free will.

2. Our trials are always shared with us by Christ.

There it is for us to read and believe: *"Surely He has borne our griefs and carried our sorrows."* Isaiah 53:4. It must be of some comfort to all of us to know that whatever our grief, whatever our sorrow will be — it is shared with us by Christ.

- Financial collapse
- The illness of one of our beloved children
- The agony of an unwanted divorce
- Prolonged bouts of depression
- Living daily with chronic pain
- Grieving over the sudden passing away of a precious loved one
- The inability to accept the limitations of aging or illness

It must be of some comfort to know *that very sorrow, that very grief is shared with us by Christ.*

One of my favorite promises of Scripture is this: *"I am with you."* In fact, I'm more and more convinced that this simple promise from the Father is the central, the most consistent, the most frequent promise in the entire Bible. It is perhaps most familiar to us in Psalm 23:4:

> *"Yea, though I walk through the valley of the shadow*
> *of death, I fear no evil; For You are with me...."*

In their zeal to win others to Christ, many pastors, evangelists, and lay Christians have painted a picture of the Christian life that doesn't exist: a life of success, of health and prosperity, of one delightful experience after another. I've never read a Scripture verse that says the Christian life is a life of ease. Accordingly, I believe that "selling" Christianity in such a way robs Scripture of its integrity and cheats the prospective convert of the Truth. Selling a potential convert to Christianity on an illusion will only lead to disillusion when he finds out for himself the truth about the Christian life.

What is the truth about the Christian life? The truth is that conversion to Christ is not the point at which all problems cease; in a very real sense, it is the place where often real challenges and heartbreaks begin. The Christian life is often one of valleys, deep pits, and dark shadows of discouragement, loneliness, and betrayal. You may be experiencing this reality of the Christian life right now. But praise God for His promise: *"Thou art with me."* Christ is right here with us, sharing in our suffering.

3. God wants to transform our trials into ministries of compassion for others.

We have a great privilege when a trial enters our life, to become imitators of Christ by using our wounds and suffering as a source of healing love for others.

The Wounded Healer by Henri Nouwen has affected my attitude toward trials more than any other book. In that book, Nouwen writes:

> *"All of our witness, all of our service, all our good intention for Christ will never be perceived as authentic until it comes from a heart that is wounded."*

Nouwen's challenge is this: We must learn to take our trials, our broken relationships, our low self-esteem, our illness, or whatever our brokenness is, and let God transform it. We must become so open and vulnerable with others about those wounds that they can be used as a source of healing power in broken lives.

Let me give you an example from the life of a good friend of mine. Diane Schmidt was a wounded healer. After suffering a sore throat for a period of weeks, Diane went to a doctor who told her she needed to have her tonsils out. One tonsil was removed and was found to be tumorous. The tumor was malignant, and there was a question as to whether or not the malignancy was spreading throughout her lymphatic system.

I sat with Diane in the hospital room when the doctor came in and outlined her alternatives. In a very loving but forthright manner Diane said, "I want you to know first of all, Doctor, that I am a Christian. Because I'm a Christian, my life is in God's hands and I know that even if this cancer ends my life, I will live with Him in eternity."

The doctor then went through the options, the best of which seemed to be immediate surgery. She said, "That's fine, let's do the surgery." The next day, Diane spent ten hours in surgery. I was with her mother and sister in the waiting room those ten hours. Finally the physician came out and said, "I just want you to know that in all the years I've been a surgeon, I have never seen a woman with such character in suffering as Diane."

Until the day of her death, Diane lived her life as a wounded healer. On the night before her death, I invited Diane to share her testimony at Forest Home Christian Conference Center, which she did with grace and courage.

All of us have wounds, all of us have trials. The call of God is to be so open and vulnerable about those wounds that they can be used as a source of healing to other brokenhearted people. Who ministers to the alcoholic better than someone who has struggled with the same disease? Who ministers to the cancer patient better than someone who has struggled with the same disease? Think of the struggles and trials you have undergone, or that you are undergoing now. Who is better equipped to understand and minister to someone who hurts in those same ways than you?

If you hide your hurt and hold it inside, it becomes unbearable pain, serving no purpose, comforting no one, helping no one. But if you learn to turn your suffering into service to others, you can rejoice and give glory to God.

The words of Father Van in his book, *The Son's Cause,* have guided me throughout my life:

> *"To turn a small trial into a trough of self-pity is to make it and ourselves more petty. To share it with Him is to turn it, however small it may be, into a thing of grandeur — a giving of love to others."*

4. When there has been a season of extreme trial, there often must be given significant time for healing.

If we have a loved one who is walking through a valley of great darkness, I want to encourage us to not charge into that person's life with words of unsolicited advice or cherry clichés. Often, the way we can help most is simply by our presence and our prayers.

Again, I turn to Henri Nouwen who writes wisely:

> *"The friend who can be silent with us in a moment of despair or confusion, who can stay with us in an hour of grief and bereavement, and face with us the reality of our struggles — this is a friend who truly cares."*

This fourth principle is particularly helpful when seeking to care for the friend or family member who has lost a loved one.

At times, when a loved one is recovering from the loss of a cherished family member, the person may even go through a period of doubt. In the classic book, A Grief Observed, C.S. Lewis bluntly recorded his feelings of anger over the loss of his wife to cancer:

> *"Her absence is like the sky, spread over everything. Where is God? Go to Him when your need is desper-*

ate, when all others help in vain, and what do you find? A door slammed in your face, and a sound of bolting and double bolting on the inside. After that, silence."

For Lewis it took a long time before he returned to a strong and vital faith, now deeper than ever before. He was able to find healing for the great trials through the support of some loving friends who gave him time to recover.

1. **The vast majority of trials that enter our lives can be at least partially understood if we grasp the Biblical Doctrine of Free Will**
2. **Our trials are always shared with us by Christ**
3. **God wants to transform our trials into ministries of compassion for others.**
4. **When there has been a season of extreme trial, there often must be given significant time for healing.**

These four principles guided me throughout my life as I have faced various trials and sought to minister to others who are facing life's greatest heartaches.

Joe Bayly tells of an experience he had in a time of trial, shortly after his five-year-old son died of leukemia. It was a windy, below-zero Saturday morning in January, and there was more than a foot of snow on the ground. Looking out the window of his home, Bayly saw the postal truck pull up to his mailbox. Without pausing to put on a coat, he ran out of the house, took the mail out of the box, and was about to rush back into the house when something among the letters caught his attention: a colorfully printed seed catalog.

On the front of the catalog were brilliant zinnias; on the back, luscious red tomatoes. Standing in his shirtsleeves, Bayly seemed not to even notice the cold as he leafed through the pages of roses, daffodils, dahlias, marigold, corn, peas and cucumbers. The fragrances of springtime seemed to rise from the pages, and for a brief moment the winter was past and he felt warmed and cheered.

Then the cold wind whipped up around him, and he rushed back inside and closed the door behind him. Bayly later reflected on how our experiences as Christians are like that moment at the mailbox. "We feel the cold," he wrote, "just as those who do not share our hope, the biting wind that penetrates us as it penetrates them. But in our cold times, we have a seed catalog called The Bible. We open it, and we smell the promised spring, the eternal spring, and the first fruit that settles our hope is Jesus Christ, who was raised from death and cold earth to glory-eternal."

That is what the Christian life is like — a fragrance of Christ and the coming spring amid the wintry trials of life.

Our lives are just a gleam of time between two Eternities — but God is at work in our lives to fan that gleam into a shining glory, the glory of His own reflected image. The choice is ours: we can surrender to the cold and darkness of our trials — or we can allow God's light and warmth to shine through our lives in spite of our trials.

Chapter 11

CHOOSING JOY WHEN ANGER AND DEPRESSION TOUCH OUR LIVES

Beth was a Christian woman who seemingly never got angry. Her kind and sweet disposition was well-known to everyone throughout the church where she was an active member. Over the years, no one had ever seen this lovely lady become angry with anyone, until one day in the midst of a mild disagreement with a neighbor, this apparently gracious woman took a bottle of carbolic acid and threw it into the face of her neighbor. Her neighbor was permanently scarred and partially blinded.

After prolonged Christian counsel, Beth came to realize that her tragic over-reaction was caused, in part, due to years and years of repressed anger. Beth had grown up in a conservative Christian home and church environment where she was taught that it was a sin to ever get angry. Pressed down, month after month, year after year, finally her anger exploded one day in a way that would affect her neighbor for the rest of her life.

Author Ann Kiemel was picked up at the airport by a married couple, friends she hadn't seen since college. In their arms they carried Paula, their little girl, who had braces on her legs, the result of cerebral palsy. As they were getting into the car, Paula climbed into Ann's lap and said, "Ann, I have a new baby brother."

Seeing no baby, Ann asked, "Where is he?"

Paula's mother, Margie, turned around from the front seat and said, "Ann, Paula doesn't understand. God did give us a little baby boy a few months ago, but he only lived for a few weeks."

She went on to explain that after their baby died, they became angry with God. They asked Him, "*Why* did this happen? *Why* was this baby born perfect and healthy and normal, only to die a few weeks later from a sudden and unexpected respiratory infection? *Why* was he snatched from us so suddenly?"

"Ann," she concluded, "we still don't have all the answers, but we're working it through. Our anger and our pain have gradually been replaced by His peace. Even though we don't understand why He took our baby away, we do understand that He's given us a ministry to other parents who have lost little babies. He's given us a ministry to other parents of children with cerebral palsy, like Paula. We're reaching scores of people for Christ who could never have been reached otherwise, and we're thankful to God for that."

Beth and Margie, two women with two dramatically different responses toward anger. The New Testament is filled with admonitions about anger. Implicit throughout these admonitions is the basic assumption that we will have natural feelings of anger — that anger, even in the life of the Christian, is to be expected. In Ephesians 4:26, the apostle Paul gives us a twofold piece of advice, beginning with a quote from Psalm 4:4: *"In your anger, do not sin."* Then he concludes in his own words, *"Do not let the sun go down while you are still angry."*

Over the years there has been some confusion over this verse because some versions translate those first words of Ephesians 4:26 something like "Be angry, and sin not." Note that this is not a command that we are to build anger into our character; rather, this is simply Paul's acknowledgement that we will sometimes have feelings of anger. The New International Version makes this clear: *"In your anger, do not sin."*

The rest of that verse advises, *"Do not let the sun go down while you are still angry."* Don't let your natural feelings of anger turn into sin; don't let too much time go by without positively *resolving* those feelings of anger. Throughout the Scriptures there is an implicit acknowledgement that all of us will have angry feelings toward other people at times. How we choose to respond to those natural feelings of anger will determine whether we have acted sinfully or righteously.

Jesus took the subject of anger very seriously. In the Sermon on the Mount He said, *"You have heard that it was said to the people long ago, 'Do not murder, and anyone who murders will be subject to judgement.' But I tell you that anyone who is angry with his brother will be subject to judgement."*

But Jesus, like Paul, recognizes that moments of provocation are inevitable in life, and He shows us what our response should be when our anger is provoked: We must seek reconciliation and forgiveness with the person who has angered us. "First go and be reconciled to your brother; then come and offer your gift." If we are unwilling to forgive one another and deal with our anger positively and constructively, then our religious acts mean nothing.

Three principles related to anger have guided me throughout my life:

1. We need to take personal ownership for our anger.

I seek to never blame my anger onto someone else. I have attempted to always teach my children and grandchildren to say, "I feel angry" rather than "You make me angry." An emotionally healthy person will seek to take ownership for his or her feelings.

Noted author Bruce Larson wrote before his death, *"No one makes you angry. You are not someone else's victim."* Psychotherapist Fritz Perls wrote these words:

> *"Conventional psychology, which often teaches that you are a victim of what your parents or others have done to you, is a disease masquerading as a cure."*

Another Christian psychologist puts it this way:

> *"There is only one type of person with whom I counsel who I do not believe will ever get better: the person who blames others for his or her problems."*

We need to take ownership of our anger.

2. The anger we feel needs to be directed toward the problem, not the person.

The wise Christian learns to say to his loved ones, "I'm feeling some anger toward something that is happening *between us*." The goal of the mature Christian in relationship with his loved ones is to seek to form a *partnership* so that we together can confront the problem that is creating tension between us. Accordingly, now the anger is not addressed toward the person. Now the anger is addressed toward the problem, and we, in loving partnership, seek to bring resolution and healing. I have found this principle especially helpful as a parent, as through the years I have formed partnerships with my children, Rachael and Nathan.

3. As we acknowledge anger within us, we can decide what our response to the anger will be: Repress, Express or Confess.

In my view, and in the view of many, two extreme positions are often taken in relationship to anger. Within the institutional church, very often the subtle or overt message has been to repress all anger. This false teaching suggests that Christians are to never get angry. We need to understand that this cognitive error often leads to all sorts of other emotional and relational problems.

The second extreme which is taught within certain segments of contemporary culture is to ventilate, to explode when you are angry regardless of the pain this may instill in others. Carol Tavris, in her excellent book entitled, *Anger: The Misunderstood Emotion* confronts head-on this second option of the unrestrained expression of anger as "one of today's most accepted myths of popular psychology." Tavris refers to multiple clinical studies that clearly demonstrate that unrestrained expression of anger (screaming, verbal abuse, yelling, etc.) tends to *increase*, not reduce anger. Tavris concludes that the open expression of anger actually stimulates rather than reduces anger feelings. This, in turn, raises blood pressure and adrenaline levels, and the result is greater physical stress and risk to health. Tavris cites study after study to confirm these conclusions.

I submit that often there is a third option, a third way, for the

Christian. This third path in response to anger is confession, where we are experiencing such a vital, winsome, growing walk with God that throughout the day, we can go to the Heavenly Father and share our hearts:

> *"Loving God, I come to you to tell you of my hurt and anger. I need your wisdom to know if this is just something petty that I need to give up to you now, or if this is something where I need to go to a loved one and seek to form a partnership so that we can come to resolution."*

By way of personal witness, this third principle has been the most helpful to me as I wrestle with feelings of hurt and anger.

As you probably know, anger that is not appropriately resolved can lead to prolonged depression. Furthermore, we have an increasing body of evidence that suggests that repressed anger and depression can lead adults and adolescents to acting out and addictive behaviors. This is a topic that potentially touches every family, often with deeply tragic consequences.

Seven primary symptoms are frequently associated with depression. These are traits that caring Christians need to remember both for their own lives and as they are building compassionate relationships with others:

1. Difficulty concentrating and/or making decisions
2. Ongoing fatigue and/or decreased energy
3. Insomnia, early morning wakefulness or excessive sleeping
4. Loss of interest in activities or hobbies that were once pleasurable
5. Overeating or appetite loss
6. Persistent feelings of hopelessness, sadness or despair
7. Gradual isolation from loved ones, family and friends

I have found it helpful to distinguish between situational depression and clinical (sometimes referred to as chronic) depression. Perhaps all of us have battled with situational depression. A situation arises in our lives: divorce, our children leaving home, serious illness, chronic pain, aging, financial crisis, the death of a loved one, etc., and we acknowledge that these situations lead us into depression. I have confronted several seasons of situational depression in my own life. By way of personal witness, three decisions that helped me more than any other choices as I walked through these valleys were:

- To maintain a warm, daily walk with Jesus Christ
- To initiate close contact with family and beloved friends
- To exercise daily

Clinical depression, in contrast to situational depression, is generally distinguished by these six characteristics:

1. Symptoms continue even when life situation improves (for example, when a person heals from a physical illness but symptoms of depression continue, this may be a sign of clinical depression.)
2. There is no apparent cause for the depression (this can be caused by changes in the hormonal or neurological systems).
3. There are frequent thoughts of suicide.
4. There is a family history of clinical depression.
5. Clinical depression is recognized as more severe and prolonged than situation depression.
6. Clinical depression causes greater impairment in functioning. The person often becomes completely immobilized and totally unable to make daily decisions.

I'm certain that each of you reading this chapter regularly minster to other people. It is my encouragement to all of us to know the symptoms of depression and to ask God to give us wisdom to guide us as we care for one another. This includes the option of referring a person to a competent Christian therapist. With God's help, and the unconditional love of a friend, even a person profoundly struggling with anger and depression can rediscover a life of joy.

Chapter 12

CHOOSING JOY BY EXPERIENCING FREEDOM FROM TOXIC SHAME

Linda was a vivacious, outgoing, attractive 19-year old Christian woman. She became pregnant. She was unmarried. When she shared the news of her pregnancy with her boyfriend, and of her decision that she was unwilling to have an abortion, he left her. Next, Linda shared with her parents, members of a rigid, legalistic church. They reprimanded her, "You have ruined our testimony in our church. We are so ashamed of you." Then they disowned her.

Despite the cruel rejection, Linda was determined to have her child. Several months later she gave birth to a beautiful baby boy named "Steven". Linda loved little Steven with all her heart. She read all the books she could find on how to be a good parent, and every free hour she had after working all day, she tenderly spent with her little son.

One day a neighbor lady was coming up the stairs of the apartment complex where Linda lived. As she approached the section of the apartment building near Linda's unit, she heard sobbing. Noticing the front door was ajar, the lady made her way into Linda's apartment. She quickly walked toward the family room where she found Linda, her hair covering her face, tears streaming down her cheeks. Linda's hands were tightly gripped around the neck of her little baby. She was strangling little Steven to death. Fortunately, the neighbor lady had arrived just in time to pull Linda off the little boy — and his life was saved after a prolonged period of hospitalization.

Everyone who knew Linda was surprised by her action. She loved Christ, and she loved her baby with all her heart. Through the long and often painful hours of Christian therapy, Linda came to the realization that her action of great brokenness in attempting to strangle her baby was rooted in deep-seeded shame. Linda felt so ashamed of herself. She had been so shamed by her parents. She felt so ashamed of what God must be feeling toward her for having become pregnant and unmarried that she concluded she was deserving of nothing so wonderful as a little boy. So, in an act of great emotional turmoil, she attempted to take little Steven's life.

Fortunately, there is a happy ending to this story. Linda met and married a Christian man, and he adopted little Steven. Today, years later, Linda and her husband and Steven are a happy family. However, to this day, Linda continues to go through a long process of discovering healing from the shame that binds her.

Shame wears many faces, and it stalks every one of us. Yet, when we think of shame, we hardly ever think of Jesus, do we?

The French Monastic Reformer, Bernard of Clairvaux, reminds us that Christ identifies with our shame in a hymn familiar to some of us: *"Oh Sacred Head now wounded, with grief and shame weighed down."* Even though we may have sung these words before, have we ever really reflected on the phrase, *"grief and shame weighed down"*? Do we understand that Bernard of Clairvaux did not just conjure up in his mind the idea that Jesus perhaps felt shame? No, he found that idea in Scripture. Hebrews 12:2 reads, *"Looking unto Jesus, the author and finisher of our faith, who for the joy that was set before him, endured the cross, despising the shame, and is now seated at the right hand of God, the Father."* More than anyone, Christ identifies with our struggles with shame.

There is a type of agony attached to shame that is unlike any other emotion. Christian psychologists teach us shame can often be an even more devastating struggle than guilt. Sometimes it is hard for us, or for our loved ones to even go on in life in the midst of our shame because there is always this accuser saying to us, either from another person or within our own mind, "You are flawed. You are defective. You are inadequate. You are deficient. You ought to be ashamed of yourself."

Throughout the seasons of life, shame pursues us — and it pursues our loved ones.

Shame stalks the one who knows that he has in his past demeaned his own child. Physically, or psychologically, or verbally, he has abused his own son or daughter. Very often he was abused as a child and that cycle has continued — and in that cycle, there is shame.

Shame is often felt by those who have been through the pain of divorce. Particularly it stalks the woman who attends an unloving and rigid church. Against her will and against her wishes, her husband has left her for another. Yet as she dresses to attend worship on a Sunday morning, she feels ashamed because she knows that as she comes to church, she wears the label "divorced" — and accompanying that label, there is shame.

Shame can touch the person who finds herself or himself physically overweight. In this culture that worships the god of physical appearance, shame stalks the obese person.

Shame weighs down heavily upon the young woman who grew up in a home where mom or dad or both were alcoholics. There was this hidden life the girl lived out daily. When she went to school or church, outwardly everything was wonderful. But when she went home, home was no haven. It felt more like hell. Now, years later, even though she wasn't the alcoholic — it was her mom and dad — she is the one who feels ashamed about that reality. We know psychologically this is often true.

Shame relentlessly pursues the woman who sits across from me at a Starbucks. She tells me she weighs nearly 300 pounds. She goes on to share, "I've learned through Christian therapy that I gained all this weight because my stepdad sexually abused me as a child. Again. And again. And again. And so as a defense mechanism, I thought that if I could just put on all this weight, Ron, that I'd never be desirable again to my stepdad or to any man." Then, she weeps, and in that weeping there is shame.

Shame can impact the young boy in a family whose older brother has excelled in sports. The first born son has great talent, and the last born often feels "I'll never measure up to him. The expectations for me are high, but I feel inadequate to succeed to the degree my brother has performed." The young boy feels ashamed of who he is, and the lack of what he is able to accomplish athletically. As a child and adolescent, I often felt this sense of shame.

Shame pursues the young woman who as a child was told by mom or dad: "You're stupid!" "You will never amount to anything!" "You are lazy!" "You ought to be ashamed of yourself!" Now years or even decades later, the woman carries that childhood shame with her despite the reality that she is living out a meaningful and compassionate life.

I declare to all of us the Good News of the Gospel: *"There is now therefore no shame for those of us who are in Christ Jesus."* (Romans 8:1)

The Greek term used in this verse, which is often translated, "condemnation" (katakrino) carries with it the worst kind of shaming. Some of you, and some of your loved ones, have lived with it all your life. The Good News of the Gospel is that there is now no *katakrino*, no shaming for those of us who are in Christ Jesus.

Two principles to guide us as we wrestle with shame:

1. **Those who are not qualified to shame you, often will. Refuse to give them the power to shame you ever again.**

Some of you may be in very shame-based environments. In the past, in those shameful-oriented situations, perhaps you've given people the power to shame you. The Good News of the Gospel challenges you: *Refuse to give those people the control over you ever again!*

For many years, Marjorie was stalked by shame. She shared with a pastor friend of mine that when she was in the third grade, she had been reprimanded by her teacher for some minor act of misbehavior. Her teacher, a harsh, vindictive, shame-based disciplinarian called Marjorie to stand in front of the class. The teacher then commanded, "Children, I want each of you to come to the blackboard and write a negative sentence that begins with the word 'Marjorie'. Write something you dislike about this disobedient girl."

One after another, the students came forward writing on the blackboard hurtful statements like, "Marjorie is ugly." "Marjorie is stupid." "Marjorie has no friends." "Marjorie is fat." The third graders wrote sentence after sentence until all twenty-five students had filled the blackboard. As Marjorie shared this story with my pastor friend, she began to cry.

My friend then spoke gently to Marjorie. He said, "I want you to picture that classroom again, but now visualize a 26th student in the room. His name is Jesus. After all the other classmates have written their cruel words with their chalk, Jesus stands and instead of picking up the chalk, he picks up the eraser. He then quietly walks to the front of the class and wipes the board clean. Now he takes the chalk and begins to write, "Marjorie is beloved." "Marjorie is my child." "Marjorie is beautiful." "Marjorie is forgiven." "Marjorie is unconditionally loved."

On that day, Marjorie began to find healing from the shame that bound her.

Those who are not qualified to shame you, will. Through Christ, refuse to give them the power to do so.

2. **The only one who is qualified to shame you never will. Stay close to Him. Stay close to a Christ who wants to value you, not shame you, who wants to trade in that shame for grace.**

Many years ago, a young woman who was a member of our

church came into my office to share her life story with me. Nancy had given her life to Christ, but still battled the shame from her past. For years, she had been involved in a whole series of illicit affairs with married men. She was very ashamed of her past life, and she had discussed this struggle with me many times. So, I will always remember the day she burst into my office and joyfully proclaimed, "Ron, I have to tell you something. I've discovered that in God's sight, I'm a virgin!" Then Nancy began to read to me scriptures she had discovered.

> *"As far as the east is from the west, so far have I removed your transgression from you."*
> Psalm 103:12

> *"I will remember your sin no more."*
> Hebrews 10:17

> *"We will become in Him as white as snow."*
> Isaiah 1:18

> *"If we confess our sins, He is faithful and just to forgive us our sins, and to cleanse us from all unrighteousness."*
> 1 John 1:9

Nancy found freedom from her shame.

Believe with me this Great Truth: *"There is now therefore no shame for those of us who are in Christ Jesus."* When we truly experience this reality in our hearts, the result will be a life of greater joy!

Chapter 13

CHOOSING JOY THROUGH BUILDING AUTHENTIC FRIENDSHIPS

During my childhood, adolescent and young adult years, one of my favorite actors was William Holden. I especially remember his performances in *The Bridge on the River Kwai, The Towering Inferno,* and *Love Is a Many Splendored Thing.* There was a season in his life when William Holden was a beloved friend to many. He was particularly close to fellow actor Ronald Reagan, and served as the best man at Reagan's wedding.

However, as Holden aged, he began a journey into increasing isolation — a tendency which is sadly characteristic of many men and women in their second half of life. In November of 1981, the L.A. Times printed the following account of the actor's death:

> *"William Holden was a very private man, and he died a very private death. Alone in his apartment in Santa Monica, he bled to death from a gash in his forehead, caused by a drunken fall against his bedside table. It was four or five days later that his body was found. He was 63 years old."*

I was surprised when I first read this account. Here was a man who had for four decades been starring in blockbuster hit films. Yet when he dies, no one apparently had reached out to him for several days. We get a clue to this presumed mystery where we read the final sentence of this news account: "William Holden guarded his privacy with increasing vigilance."

Many in our culture today are guarding their privacy with increasing vigilance. We may be choosing more and more to be alone, to pull back from even our own family and friends. Indeed, recent comprehensive sociological research indicates that the proportion of adults with no close friends has tripled since 1985. We may be moving into increased isolation, yet when we open scripture, we come to understand that isolation is an enemy, particularly as we seek to joyfully age. The Bible guides us to an understanding that we are created to be in relationship — with our loving God and with one another as friends.

In John 15:12-17, we discover a manifesto on friendship given to us by Jesus. In this crucial teaching, our Lord gives us two characteristics that will be essential for the friendships we seek out in our lives:

First, our true friends will have a disregard for personal sacrifice. Jesus, on the night before the cross, said to his disciples, *"Greater love hath no man than this, that a man lay down his life for his friends."*

We need to be very discerning in how we interpret this verse. I believe, as do most Bible scholars, that the primary teaching of this verse is that Jesus is teaching us about the approaching cross. So on the night he was betrayed, he said to his disciples and to us in essence, *"I'm about to lay down my life for you — that is how great my love is for you."* But I also believe, as do most Bible interpreters, that there is a secondary meaning here: that there is, in fact, a universal Christian principle given to us in John 15:13, and that principle is that what God expects of us is a willingness to lay down our lives for those we love.

In the aftermath of the horrific mass shooting in San Bernardino on December 2, 2015, Denise Paraza tells a moving story. As 60 rounds of bullets were being sprayed across a room at the Inland Regional Center, Denise's friend Shannon Johnson wrapped his arms around Denise to protect her from the terrorists. Denise later said, *"I will always remember his left arm wrapped around me, holding me as close as possible next to him behind a chair. I'll always remember him saying three words over and over again: 'I got you. I got you. I got you.' This amazing man layed his life down for me. He died so that I could live."*

At the memorial service for Shannon Johnson, the pastor read

114

from John 15:13, *"Greater love hath no man than this, that a man lays down his life for his friend."*

Charles Dickens, in his novel *A Tale of Two Cities*, writes of such a friendship between two men, Charles Darnay and Sidney Canton. Darnay is a Frenchman, and has been thrown into the dungeon, awaiting execution on the guillotine. Canton is a burnt-out physician, living a wild and decadent life. He hears word that his friend Darnay is about to be executed. That night he slipped into the prison and exchanged clothes with Darnay. Darnay escaped that night, and the next morning, Canton took his place. As he walked up to the scaffold and stood before the guillotine to have his life taken from him, he said these words: "I see the lives for which I now lay down my life, in that England which I shall see no more. It is a far, far better thing I do than I have ever done. It is a far, far greater rest that I go to than I have ever known." And then Canton died for his friend. Charles Dickens then quotes from John 15:13, *"Greater love hath no man than this, that a man lay down his life for his friends."*

Lyman Coleman tells of a time a number of years ago when he was meeting with eighteen Presbyterian elders from the same church. They were gathered in a big circle in a meeting room. He said, "Suppose that it's 3:00 a.m. and you can't sleep. You have a problem on your heart and mind, you're unable to sleep. You know that you can make only one phone call, and so you want to call a person who you know would understand, who would listen, who would care, who would be there for you, who wouldn't be upset that even in the middle of the night you've caused the inconvenience of waking them up. Who would you call?"

They began to go around the room, and the first elder said, "Well, I'd call an old army buddy. We went through a lot together. I know he'd always be there for me." The second elder said, "Well, there are a couple of fraternity brothers I know. I'd call one of them.

They're great friends to me." The third elder said, "Well, there's an old high school friend. We've stayed in touch through the years. I'd call him." And on they went around the room until all eighteen had shared. And when they had concluded their sharing, not one of them had shared anyone in the church of which they were a part, let alone that group of elders as they met together in the room. Then Lyman Coleman said, "It would seem to me that if there was one place on this earth where there ought to be that kind of 3:00 a.m. Christian love, it ought to be lived out in our Christian communities."

I am deeply grateful to have had a number of friends in my life whom I know without question would lay down their lives for me, as I would for them. Our true friends will have a disregard for personal sacrifice.

Second, our true friends will be dedicated to mutual goals. In John 15:14, Jesus says, *"You are my friends if you do what I command you."* It may be of interest to you that in the New Testament Greek text the verb tense is present. So the passage could be faithfully translated: *"You are my friends, if you keep on doing what I have commanded you."* Our true friends will be dedicated to mutual good.

Dr. Dan Buettner has written an excellent best-selling book entitled *The Blue Zones*. In this book, Buettner sketches in for us the five communities in the world where the *average* life span of the citizens is nearly 100. From his research, he then shares the common characteristics found in these diverse communities.

One of the most significant traits discovered in all these villages was: *they surrounded themselves with friends who shared their values.* In other words, there was a dedication to mutual goals. Dr. Buettner writes, "Prolonged research found that people with the strongest social connection with friends who shared their values lived significantly longer. Those with the least social connectedness were two to three times more likely to die over a period of years than those with several close friends."

Dr. Dean Ornish, one of the finest integrative physicians in the United States writes:

> *"In my book, Love and Survival, I summarized literally hundreds of studies showing that people who feel lonely and isolated are many times more likely to die prematurely than those who are closely bonded with family and friends. Not only from coronary heart disease, but from virtually all causes of premature death. We sometimes can view the time we spend forging out friendships as luxuries that we do only after the important stuff in our lives is done. Yet, research makes it clear that this is the 'important stuff.'"*

Clearly, a significant body of research indicates that the way you answer the question, "how are you fixed for friends?" will play an important part in the likelihood of future health and longevity.

One of the most meaningful experiences of my life has been to be a part of a men's accountability group. In this type of small group, several men covenant to vulnerably share their lives together as they meet weekly. My beloved friend, Dave Barry wrote to me some time ago about what our group meant to him:

> *"Ron, through our men's accountability group meetings over many years, we grew to become extremely close friends. In our group of Christian brothers, we supported each other when our men lost jobs, went through divorces, battled addictions, struggled with depression and went through seasons of doubt over their Christian faith. We supported the family as one of our group members went home to be with God. We*

knew what we shared in our group stayed in our group, and this deep trust allowed us to admit our failures and shortcomings — and to be held accountable to become better men for Christ."

What Dave Barry and the other friends in our group all shared together was *a dedication to mutual goals.*

When my brother Paul was diagnosed with a rapidly spreading cancer that would take his life at the age of 41, both Paul and I relied upon family and friends to help sustain us. I frequently flew from my California home to Denver to be with my brother in the final weeks of his life. Often, I slept overnight in his hospital room with him on a spare bed graciously provided to me. After his death, I flew to Denver to support his wife and two young sons and to help plan the memorial service which I would lead. During those days, I was in frequent contact with three friends who lived in California. When they called one day, I asked how things were going back home. To my complete surprise, they said, "Actually, Ron, we're not calling from California. We're calling from a motel in Denver. We flew in last night just to be here to support you in any way we can in the days ahead." I wept as I experienced the deep love of these friends for me and my family in a time of devastating loss.

I truly believe with all my heart that on the night when Jesus was betrayed, that when he said, "Greater love hath no man than this, that a man lays down his life for his friends" — these words were not just beautiful, sentimental prose. Rather, these words were an expectation of the way we could come to love one another as Christian friends. As we share that love with our friends, we discover in our heart a great sense of joy.

Chapter 14

CHOOSING JOY AS WE INVEST OUR LIVES IN OTHERS

Ken Heileger was a lifelong mentor to me. He began investing in my life when I was nine years old and continued to invest his life in me until his death. Ken was my Sunday school teacher in fourth, fifth, and sixth grades. He had some unorthodox teaching methods, such as rewarding his students with a nickel, dime or quarter for memorizing scripture. He was a tremendous model of Christian love.

Throughout my junior high and high school years, Ken never missed a sporting event or choir concert in which I or one of his other students participated. And even into my college years, Ken sent me notes and letters with a specially selected verse of scripture, and often included a check for $5 or $10 to help with my expenses. Ken had such an impact on my life that I asked him to speak in both my ordination and installation services when I served in my first church.

Ken and his wife, Ann, never had children of their own, but in a very real way they've had hundreds of children. If you would have stepped into Ann's kitchen before her death, you would have seen dozens of photos taped onto the walls and the refrigerator —photos of young adults Ken and Ann had mentored. While others may have diplomas and certificates of special recognition on their office walls, Ken's office was filled with pictures of men and women to whom he had given his time and energy. Ken Heileger was a master mentor!

My dictionary gives this definition of a mentor:
Men' • tor / *n*. 1. A trusted counselor or guide. 2. a teacher or coach

This definition calls a mentor "a trusted counselor or guide." Underscore that word *trusted*. A mentor earns respect and trust by the quality and genuineness of his or her life. Further, this definition suggests that a mentor is a teacher or coach. In my experience, one specific kind of coach captures a crucial dimension of what it means to be a mentor: a *player-coach*.

A number of years ago when I was a Bible teacher for the Minnesota Vikings, I got to see a real player-coach in action: my friend

Jeff Siemon. He then played middle linebacker for the Vikings and called signals for every defensive play. Because he was a player-coach, Jeff didn't just bark orders from the sidelines. He didn't have to shout, "Hustle! Hit harder! Move left! Go downfield!" because he was right there on the field, leading by his own example. He demonstrated by his own courage what it means to hustle, to make the right moves, to be mentally agile in the clinches, to be focused on the goal.

Jeff is a player-coach-mentor off the field as well as on. He's a man of deep Christian faith and character, and many people have been attracted to Jesus Christ by the genuineness of his life and testimony. Jeff exemplifies one who stays at your side, not on your back. He inspires your best performance by his own example. To me, that's what being a mentor is all about.

If I were writing my own dictionary, I would define mentoring this way:

Men' • tor • ing / n. A process of opening our lives to others, of sharing our lives with others; a process of living for the next generation.

In many ways, the history of the highest, most enduring achievements of our culture is also a history of the mentoring process. Only in our own century has mentoring fallen into such disuse — and our society has paid a price for it. In our time, we have witnessed a gradual but steady breakdown of character, families, the work ethic and human kindness. I'm convinced that much of this social disintegration can be traced to our neglect of the mentoring process.

If you are planting for a year, plant grain.
If you are planting for a decade, plant trees.
If you are planting for a century, plant people.

Wherever we see lives being changed and Christian values being advanced, we usually find that a mentoring process is at the heart of that transformation.

From the life and example of Christ, we derive the fundamental concept of mentoring:

More time spent with fewer people equals greater lasting impact for God.

Moses mentored Joshua. Naomi mentored her daughter-in-law, Ruth. Ezra mentored Nehemiah. Elijah mentored Elisha. Elizabeth mentored her cousin, Mary. Barnabas mentored Paul and John Mark. Paul mentored his spiritual son, Timothy. Paul also mentored Priscilla and Aquila, who in turn mentored Apollos.

Jesus transformed the world because he poured his life into the Twelve. Though he preached to the masses, he invested himself in a few, knowing that those few would invest themselves in still others, and thus transform the world. If we want to transform our families, our churches, our communities, and ultimately our world, then we must discover what it means to pour our lives into individuals. We must learn to spend more time with the few. We must learn to live for the next generation. We must become mentors.

In my life, mentoring others has taken many different forms. For several years, I used to take all the younger staff members and interns from our church on a week-long trip to visit several different churches in Southern California. Each church has its own unique style and philosophy of ministry and after we visited with each church's staff members, we would share our impressions together as these young men and women were forging out their own understanding of Christian pastoral ministry. For many years, my long-time friend Dave Barry and I led a weekly men's accountability group in my home. We mentored each other in different dimensions of our lives together, and held each other accountable for our spiritual, fitness, relationship, financial and vocational goals. For several years, I had the privilege of meeting weekly one on one with four outstanding young men in Santa Barbara. We would study various books, read scripture together, and pray for one another as we sought to honor the truth of Proverbs 27:17: *"As iron sharpens iron, so one man sharpens another."* Presently, I'm involved in a mentoring process as I spend time one on one weekly with my four grandchildren. Mentoring takes many different forms, and I strongly encourage you to commit your life to this process of investing your life in others. It has been one of the most meaningful experiences of my life.

It seems every time I go back to my hometown of Clarinda, Iowa, people tell me how much they loved my dad, a Presbyterian pastor, and how they fondly recall the things he did to help people in the church and the community. This reality takes place even though my father passed away over forty years ago. Further, I can see that something of the Christlikeness of my father has become embedded in the lives of these people.

I remember one woman named Ruth saying to me, "Ron, after I lost my own father, I really needed a spiritual father. Your dad was always there to give me guidance when I was a newlywed. I had a lot of growing up to do during those years, but your dad counseled me and prayed with me and helped me be God's person in my marriage and with my children."

Just think of it: You and I can be immortal, not only in Eternity, but here on earth. Even after your death, you can reach out and touch unborn generations through the life of someone you have mentored. You can continue to impact countless lives, long after you have gone to be with our loving God, because you have lived the lifestyle of a mentor.

Dietrich Bonhoeffer stated it well when he wrote from a Nazi prison camp, *"A righteous person is one who lives for the next generation."*

A man named Walt had an ambition to start a Sunday school class for the kids in his neighborhood. So he started with one boy he found playing marbles on the sidewalk. "Son," he said, "I'd like you to come to a Sunday school class with me."

The boy turned his grimy face up at Walt and sneered, "No way! You won't catch me going to any Sunday school!"

"Well, we'll see," Walt said. "Say, that's a mighty pretty shooter you have there. And look at all those aggies and puries! I remember when I was a boy, walking around with a bag full of marbles rattling in my pocket. There's no better feeling than having a pocketful of marbles, is there?"

"I guess not," the boy said dubiously.

"Mind if I shoot a few, son?"

"Well, no, go ahead, mister." The boy was frankly perplexed by this grown up who admired his marbles and got down on his knees on the sidewalk and began shooting like an expert.

They played several games of marbles on the sidewalk. Finally, the boy grinned at Walt and said, "Say, mister, you're okay. Now, where was this Sunday school you wanted me to go to?"

So Walt and his young friend went through the neighborhood and gathered twelve more boys, and started a Sunday school class. Over the ensuing weeks, Walt gave himself sacrificially to those thirteen boys. They studied the Bible together, they went on hikes together, they played marbles and stickball together.

As Walt continued to pour himself into those boys, a strong bond of friendship grew between them. Eventually, a time came when the hearts of those boys were softened. Walt shared with them the good news of a man named Jesus, and the boys eagerly responded. Their lives were changed forever. They now wanted to follow the same Christ Walt followed.

Today, those boys have grown to manhood. Eleven of the thirteen went on to serve in full time vocational service for Christ. The first boy, the one Walt encountered on the sidewalk playing marbles, grew to become the chairman of the Center for Christian Leadership, a renowned author and speaker, and a mentor in his own right to hundreds of young men and women before his death in 2013. His name was Howard Hendricks.

Walt's body was laid to rest many years ago. But Walt isn't really gone. He lives on in Eternity. He lives in the lives of the thirteen individuals he mentored. And he will continue to live on in the lives of all the people who will, in turn, be mentored by them.

My old friend Bob Kraning, who for many years was the Director of Forest Home, a Christian Conference Center in southern California, writes,

> *"The ultimate success of my life will not be judged by the number of those who admire me for my accomplishments, but by the number of those who attribute their wholeness to my love for them — by the number of those who have seen their true beauty and worth in my eyes."*

From time to time, when my children were very young, I would frequently say to them:

> *"When you were born, you were crying and everybody else was happy. You want to live your life in such a way that when you die, you'll be happy and everybody else will be crying. You'll be happy because you are in Eternity with God. Everyone else will be shedding a tear because of the way you loved them and invested your life in them."*

In other words, because you were a mentor.

Chapter 15

CHOOSING JOY WHEN ILLNESS STRIKES

Christian author C.S. Lewis was a bachelor throughout most of his life. He was well into his 50's before he met Joy Davidman. They fell in love, were married and were exceedingly happy — until Lewis's new bride was diagnosed with an extremely severe type of cancer only months after their wedding.

As Joy battled her illness, Lewis did what any of us would do. He prayed for a dramatic miracle of healing. There was to be no miracle of healing.

Shortly after the death of his wife, Lewis began to write down his honest questions and feelings in a personal journal. These notes were later collected and published under a pseudonym; he was reluctant to publish them under his own name because they contained many troubled and frustrated questions. Lewis was angry with God. This book was not published under Lewis's own name until after his death; the title of the book: *A Grief Observed.*

It is, in my view, one of the classic vulnerable, authentic, devotional books of the last century.

In *A Grief Observed*, Lewis wrote that he felt God had let him down. Before his wife's death, he prayed for a miracle; no miracle came. After her death, he prayed for consolation; he felt only loneliness and grief. The questions and doubts he expressed were harsh, bitter, and deeply transparent.

However, toward the end of the book, Lewis began to see an error in this thinking. He realized that God had not let him down, that his relationship with Christ was strong. He also saw that he had been given false expectations by many well-meaning Christian friends about what the Bible does and does not promise in a time of trial, illness, or grief.

A key truth for us to grasp about healing is that disillusion is always the child of illusion. In life, in faith, in suffering, in disease, we will always become disillusioned if we have been taught an illusion.

And, we will lead others down a pathway of disillusionment if we teach them an illusion about what the Bible really teaches about healing.

The Bible contains some bold and amazing promises about the healing touch of God in times of trial. The Bible promises that God will be a very present help; that the Lord will renew our strength; that by the stripes and wounds of Jesus Christ we are healed; that if we ask, it shall be given. These are not illusionary statements; they are the rock-hard promises of God. Yet on the surface, they don't seem to square with the experiences C.S. Lewis faced, and they may not seem to square with the experience you are facing right now. You may be praying for release and healing from an illness or trial — either yours or that of someone you love — and the trial goes on and on, and your prayer for healing seems to go unanswered. How can we reconcile these crises of suffering with the promises of the Bible?

We can begin by understanding that God works in many ways; He cannot be boxed in, nor can He be steered along one single avenue of healing. We see in Scripture that His healing touch takes many different forms.

I want to suggest three different forms that God's healing love may take, three different ways in which God lovingly touches and transforms our trials and pain. For each of these forms of healing, I will give you a biblical example, and a contemporary example.

My purpose is to show us that God *always* heals, if we are faithful and flexible enough to accept the form of healing He has chosen for us or our loved ones.

1. Divine Intervention

Many people have experienced trials of terrible suffering and stress — such as an illness for which there is no known medical cure — and have suddenly seen God radically, dramatically, miraculously break through. This is *divine intervention*.

A biblical example of divine intervention is found in Mark 1:40-45. A leper came on his knees to Jesus and begged Him for healing. He was beyond the medical help of his day. He was alienated socially, but he had faith. "If You are willing," he told Jesus, "You can make me clean." Jesus, filled with compassion, replied, "I am willing." And, He touched the man, and immediately healed him of his incurable disease in a way that defies medical explanation.

A contemporary example of divine intervention occurred in the life of a friend of mine. A few years ago, she was diagnosed as having cancer. She asked the pastors and elders of our church to come and pray for her to be healed. Following the admonition of James 5:13-16, we went to her home, prayed for her, anointed her with oil, and laid hands on her. A few days later, she went back to the hospital for X-rays. To the bafflement of the doctors, the X-rays revealed that all evidence of her cancer — which had been so clear in the previous set of X-rays — had suddenly disappeared. She had been miraculously healed.

Miracles of healing occur in our time just as they did in the first century. I am an eyewitness. I disagree with a few of my Christian friends who believe that miracles of healing have passed away, that such miracles were of another era or dispensation.

When we see God heal in a way that defies natural explanation (as in the case of the leper in Mark 1:40-45, or my friend who was miraculously cured of cancer), then we are awed and humbled that God in His compassion has chosen to move in this way. Our hearts are filled with joy and gratitude. However, God does not always choose to act by this means. Let's look together at a second form of healing.

2. Partnership

There are times when God chooses not just to work for us, but with us, in partnership with the accepted medical and nutritional practices of the day. A biblical model of this second kind of healing is found in John 9. There, Jesus and his disciples came upon a man who had been blind since birth. "Rabbi," the disciples asked him, "who sinned, this man or his parents, that he was born blind?"

Jesus' reply cut through their fatalistic view of life, and dispelled the false idea that a specific incidence of suffering is always due to an act of sin: "Neither this man nor his parents sinned," said Jesus, "but [this happened so] that the works of God should be revealed in him."

Then Jesus applied a poultice of mud to the blind man's eyes, and instructed him to bathe in the pool of Siloam. This practice obviously seems ineffectual and archaic compared with modern medicine. But in full accord with the medical practices of that day, the man stepped into the pool, washed the mud form his eyes, and emerged seeing for the first time in his life. Jesus Christ, the Great Physician, worked in partnership with the medical remedy of that time, and provided the power behind the treatment that gave sight to the blind man.

Throughout the ministry of Jesus Christ, we see that He not only preached — He loved, He showed compassion, He cared for human need and suffering. That is why Jesus healed the leper, why He touched the blind man, why He ministered to the woman who was bleeding internally, and why He singled out the little children, and called them to Him.

The very presence of hospitals in Western civilization is rooted in the ministry and compassion of Jesus Christ. Before Christ, the prevailing view of life was fatalism; it said, "If you suffer, it's because of your sin. Therefore, you don't deserve medical care. You deserve your suffering." Jesus dispelled this fatalistic view of life, saying, *"I've taken your sin onto Myself. Now you must respond in a new way toward suffering. No longer should you let suffering or illness defeat you. No longer should you passively sit by and allow suffering to destroy you and those around you. I want you to fight suffering."*

I read of a little girl some time ago in a newspaper account who was fourteen years old, critically ill, on medication and receiving daily medical care from a group of outstanding physicians. The parents, well-meaning Christians, said that they believed they were being led to take her off of all medication and medical care, relying instead on faith and prayer. This had been the guidance they received from a so-called faith healer. So she was taken off all medication, and a short time later, she died. The biblical view is that we rely on faith and prayer, and we do everything we can in partnership with the medical community to see that healing comes.

For a moment, let's not confine our discussion of healing only to illness or physical injury. There is little point in praying, "Help me, Lord, to have a better self-image," or, "Help me, Lord, to become more mature in Christ," or, "Help me, Lord, to have healing in a broken relationship," if we are not willing to work in *partnership* with God to bring about that healing.

Here's the Biblical Principle: *What we pray for, we give ourselves to.* For example, if I pray each morning for God to bless me with good health so that I might be a blessing to others, then I have to do my part to pursue a healthy lifestyle. For me, this has meant daily exercise and an organic, whole food, plant based diet. *What we pray for, we give ourselves to.*

A contemporary example of healing by partnership between God and medicine comes from my own family. Our daughter Rachael was born prematurely, critically ill, and was not expected to live. When the doctors told us how sick Rachael was, we didn't just take her home and pray for a healing of dramatic divine intervention. We did everything we could to work in partnership with God to heal our daughter.

We sought the prayers of many people for her life. We had her rushed by ambulance to a special children's hospital where she could receive more specific and intensive infant care. We made over a hundred visits to the hospital, conferring with our doctor, visiting Rachael, and — when she had gained some strength and resistance — putting our hands through the rubber cuffs in the incubator and stroking her (because we had learned that even with very premature children, stroking and touching is a ministry of love that encourages healing and growth.) We sought the best Christian doctors and nurses and worked in partnership with them, and eventually — by God's grace and power and the expertise of the doctors — Rachael was healed.

Rachael's healing through our partnership with medicine was no less miraculous, was no less an act of God's grace and power, than the extraordinary healing of my friend who was cured of cancer. The healing of the blind man by collaborative means was no less a miracle than the extraordinary divine intervention that cleansed the leper. They were two different forms of healing, but they had a similar result.

Yet God does not always choose to heal by one of those two means. There is a third form of healing, the form that is inevitably the most difficult for us to accept.

3. God's Sufficient Grace

There are certain times when disease, trials, or heartaches are given to us, allowed by God for His purposes, and they are not going to be taken away. They're going to have to be endured, yet they don't have to defeat us.

The apostle Paul was able to say triumphantly, *"We are more than conquerors through Him who loved us"* (Romans 8:37), even though he suffered through a long period of physical pain and struggle in his own life. In 2 Corinthians 12, Paul referred to this period of suffering as *"a thorn in the flesh."* And, though he didn't say exactly what this thorn in his flesh was, we know it had a hindering effect on his ministry and a debilitating effect on his life. Because Paul felt that this suffering made him less effective as a man of God, he went to God the Father three times in prayer, begging God, *"Please heal me! Please remove this thorn in the flesh!"*

But God answered, *"Paul, I will give you My grace, which is sufficient for this time of trial. I will give you My strength in your weakness."* (2 Corinthians 12:7-10).

The Greek word our English Bible renders "thorn" literally means "stake", a thing that pierces and brings pain. So Paul was saying, "There is a stake in my body, causing me physical pain. I've asked God three times to take it away, but my suffering is still with me." Although we can't be sure what Paul's thorn in the flesh was, some have suggested it was lasting damage from all the scourging he endured. Others suggest it was an incurable disease — malaria, epilepsy, or some other malady. My own suspicion is that Paul was gradually going blind.

In his letter to the Galatians, Paul wrote, *"You know that because of physical infirmity I preached the gospel to you at the first. And my trial which was in my flesh you did not despise or reject, but received me as an angel of God, even as Christ Jesus.... I bear you witness that... you would have plucked out your own eyes and given them to me."* (Galatians 4:13-15). And in chapter 6, he writes, *"See with what large letters I have written to you with my own hand!"* (v. 11). Paul, who usually dictated his epistles to a "secretary", concluded the Galatian letter in his own large scrawl, writing in the kind of big letters that a person gradually going blind might use. Perhaps Paul never fully recovered from his blinding encounter with Jesus Christ on the Damascus road. We can only guess.

Whatever Paul's infirmity, whatever his thorn in the flesh, we know that Paul went before the Father and prayed for healing. We know the form of healing God gave to Paul was His sufficient grace, His strength in Paul's weakness. Did this gift of grace turn out to be the best for Paul, and for God's glory? In his life and epistles, we see that Paul became even more dependent on God, and an even more faithful follower of Jesus Christ. He was able not only to declare, but also to model for us a bold statement: *"When I am weak, then I am strong. For the power of Christ dwells in me."* (2 Corinthians 12:7-10).

There are certain trials that we are not going to be able to change. We are going to have to allow them to change us. This third form of healing is as valid an expression of the miraculous healing love of God as the first two. If we tell people only about divine intervention or partnership healing, they will become disillusioned, either gradually or suddenly, as some trial comes into their lives and is not taken away.

Each of us needs to be humble and teachable in the face of what the scriptures clearly set forth. We must have the integrity and boldness to tell others, as the Bible clearly tells us, that God's healing touch sometimes takes the form of sufficient grace, His strength in our weakness. If we have that integrity and humility as we counsel others about God's healing love, then we will no longer dole out hollow promise and illusions about healing; rather, we will have ministered the whole Word of God.

Laura Claypool, the daughter of author-pastor John Claypool, was only eight years old when she was diagnosed as having acute leukemia, a form of cancer that attacks the white blood cells. Laura's father immediately did what any father would do: he went to his knees in prayer, asking God to heal his daughter and spare her life.

The entire congregation of John Claypool's church joined in praying for Laura, by faith believing Jesus would heal her, for they had seen other dramatic healings in the life of their church. In one of his sermons before that congregation, John Claypool shared about his struggle of faith through Laura's struggle for life:

> *"There were times when Laura was hurting so intensely that she had to bite on a rag and begged me to pray to God to take away that awful pain. I would kneel down beside her bed and pray with all the faith and conviction of my soul, and nothing would happen — except the pain continued to rage on.*
>
> *Again, when she asked me in the dark of the night, 'When will this leukemia go away?'*
>
> *I answered, 'I don't know, darling, but we are doing everything we know to make that happen.'*
>
> *Then, she said, 'Have you asked God when it will go away?'*
>
> *And I said, 'Yes, you heard me pray to Him many times.'*
>
> *She persisted, 'What did He say? When did He say it would go away?'*
>
> *And, I had to admit to myself that He had not said a word. I had done a lot of talking and praying and pleading, but the response of the heavens had been silence."* From *Tracks of a Fellow Struggler*

John Claypool prayed. The congregation prayed. They looked anxiously for a sign of healing in Laura's life, either by divine intervention or by partnership between God and the best efforts that medical science could offer. But the battle was not resolved by either of these means. Laura Claypool fought a courageous battle for eighteen months, and on one stormy midwinter night, her struggle ended. The form of healing God chose for Laura was to call her home to be with Him.

For a long time afterward, John Claypool agonized over the memory of his little daughter's pain and death. But in the midst of that abysmal grief, he experienced healing from the Lord, God's grace in a grieving father's weakness. He began to see in a new and profound way that all of life is a gift. A few months after Laura's death, John Claypool was able to speak these words before his congregation:

> *"Everywhere I turn I am surrounded by reminders of Laura — things we did together, things she said, things she loved. And in the presence of the reminders, I have two alternatives: either to dwell on the fact that she has been taken away, or to focus on the wonder that she was given at all."*

Those are the only two alternatives any of us have. You may have lost a loved one, possibly a beautiful little child, like Laura Claypool. Or perhaps you have seen your children grow up and move away to a distant city. Perhaps you yourself have just moved to a new place, far from family and friends, and you're lonelier than you've ever been before. Perhaps you've just been forsaken by someone who promised to love you for the rest of your life. Whatever your struggle, you really have only two alternatives regarding these loved ones and your own loneliness or grief: you can either dwell on the fact that they have been taken away, or you can focus on the wonder that by the grace of God they were given at all.

I really believe that the only way out of the valley of sorrows is to climb the mountain of gratitude. We have to realize that all of life, for however long we have it, is a gift. We cannot earn it. Life and family and friends are gifts that have been given to us by the grace of God.

When we start to see our loved ones as unmerited gifts, then we no longer want to clutch them, smother them, possess them. Instead, we hold them with open hands, knowing they are gifts from God. This one truth has helped me more than any other in my response to loss and grief.

One of the first verses of Scripture my parents taught me was Isaiah 40:31:

> *"But those who wait on the Lord*
> *Shall renew their strength;*
> *They shall mount on wings like eagles,*
> *They shall run and not be weary,*
> *They shall walk and not faint."*

There will come trials in our lives when we will pray for healing and deliverance, and we'll wait upon the Lord, and the Lord will dramatically intervene. He will miraculously renew our strength and lift us out of our trial so that we soar like eagles, praising God as we leave our pain and sorrow below.

There will also come times when we will have to work in partnership with God to bring about healing; we'll be able to run with God, not becoming weary, doing all we can together with the Great Physician, and thanking Him for His grace.

There will also come times when all we are able to do in life is walk and not faint. We won't be able to soar; we won't be able to run. We will have to withstand a trial we cannot change. But at least we will be able to walk and, by the grace of God, not faint.

What trial are you struggling with right now? God has given you a promise of healing for that trial, and He will choose one of three ways to bring that healing about.

Those who wait upon the Lord shall renew their strength. At times they shall mount up with wings as eagles. At other times they shall run and not be weary. But at least they are always going to be able to walk and not faint. Even if we are powerless to change our burden or sorrow, pain or grief, we can still stand through the sufficient grace of Jesus Christ. And in that sufficient grace, there is joy.

Chapter 16

CHOOSING JOY AS WE REFUSE TO VIEW OURSELVES AS VICTIMS

Lauren met Greg at the university where she was majoring in the humanities. He was pre-med. Soon they fell in love and were married. They agreed on a plan whereby Lauren would set aside her studies for the next several years and would work two jobs — sixty hours a week — to support them while Greg continued his studies. Later, when Greg had completed his courses, and was making a living as a doctor, it would be Lauren's turn to go back to school to get her degree.

For six years following their marriage, Lauren loved and encouraged Greg while supporting him financially. She deferred her education, her social life, and her desire for children so that she and Greg could build their dream.

Today, Greg is a doctor with a successful practice. a thousand miles from where Lauren lives alone in a small apartment. Even before obtaining his M.D. degree, he was having an affair with another woman, and planning to take her with him to another state, where — without telling Lauren — he had arranged to serve his internship.

Lauren is divorced and saddled with debt from their broken marriage. She can't afford to return to school and can't force Greg to pay her the court-ordered divorce settlement even though he now has a six-figure annual income. Lauren is bitter, trapped by feelings of anger and betrayal. Though she wants to put Greg behind her, she finds every hour is a struggle against an all-consuming hatred. She sees herself as a victim of Greg's mistreatment.

Scott has served as a Sunday school teacher and an elder in his church. A small group in the church differs from Scott on a number of issues. One of these people heard a derogatory rumor about Scott. Without bothering to check the facts or to ask Scott about it, this man gleefully seized the opportunity to discredit Scott by spreading the rumor to others. The story was false, but the damage to Scott's reputation was done. Today Scott feels like an outcast in the church he helped build. He attends services rarely, and feels depressed and resentful when he does attend, having to sit across the aisle from those who have treated him so callously. Scott sees himself as a victim of mistreatment.

Lauren and Scott are good, caring, conscientious people who have tried to live upright lives. In return, they have been betrayed or slandered or used and tossed aside. They have been cast in the role of victims, and unless they find a way to escape that role, the hurt that was done to them once in their lives will continue to hurt them again and again.

A crucial first step in moving ourselves out of the victim role is a complete reframing of our perspective. We have to move beyond our naïve expectation that if we do good, things will turn out all right. Our perception must expand to embrace the fact that the good we do will sometimes be punished, not rewarded; that the person who tells the truth will sometimes be scorned as deceptive, that the person who deals out gentleness and understanding will often be paid back in anger and resentment. To pretend otherwise is to set ourselves up for disappointment, disillusionment, and depression.

How can you and I respond to mistreatment without falling into the victim role? First, we need to understand that there are invisible emotional ties between ourselves and the people who mistreat us. We may not be aware of these connections, but they are there all the same — and the task before us, as we seek to become emotionally whole and liberated, is to break those emotional ties.

As long as we harbor bitterness toward the person who has hurt us, we allow that person to control and victimize us. We may be carrying the memories of some mistreatment that happened ten, twenty, or thirty years ago, and the person who hurt us may even be dead — but as long as we clutch the bitterness of that mistreatment, we continue to be negatively, emotionally bound to those who hurt us. They continue to control our emotions and our responses — but only if we let them. We don't have to remain victims. We can move to a place where we are free of other people's damaging control. When we make this choice, we can transform our lives into becoming agents of joy and gratitude.

You may say, "Ron, you don't know how deeply I've been hurt. After what was done to me, I can never forgive Person X." Person X may be a cruel parent, a friend, a co-worker, or a stranger. His or her offense against you may be anything from a single insult to a child-hood full of destructive abuse. Whatever the offense, the underlying principle is the same: as long as you hold onto your bitterness, you continue to be a victim. What you are really saying is that this person victimized you in the past, continues to victimize you now, and there is nothing you will ever be able to do about it. You have accepted the victim role.

A truly Christian perspective responds by saying, "Yes, you were deeply hurt back then and there is nothing you can do to change the past. But you can change what you do *now*. That means a per-spective change. That means work and commitment on your part. It means you refuse to accept the role of a victim. You determine to wrest control of your feelings from the cruel person, and you now choose — with the help of God — to take responsibility for your own feelings and your own responses to life."

When a child is mistreated or abused, he or she is powerless, an innocent victim. But an adult has profound input over how the past will penetrate and affect the present. An adult has the power to throw off the role of "victim." When we are mistreated, you and I have a choice to accept the reality of injustice in an unjust world, and get on with our lives, or to simply accept the bitter role of victim.

When I think of someone who endured enormous mistreatment, yet who refused to accept the victim role, I think of a young man named Joseph, whose story is told in the Old Testament book of Genesis. Most of us are familiar with the story of Joseph and his famous coat, of how he was sold into slavery by his brothers, and how he eventually became the right-hand man of Pharaoh.

But, Joseph's story is much more than just an interesting tale from an ancient time. His life resonates with the same hurts that face us today. If you have ever been mistreated by a family member, if you've ever been falsely accused, if you've been misjudged and unfairly treated by an employer, if you've ever been abandoned by a friend — then you have a lot in common with Joseph.

Joseph's story begins in Genesis 37. We meet him as a seventeen-year-old youth, embroiled in family turmoil. Joseph's father Jacob indulged him as the favorite son, treating him to a pampered lifestyle symbolized by the gift of a richly ornamented robe. Joseph's ten older brothers, by contrast, were treated like hired hands.

One day, far from their father's home, the brothers seized Joseph and threw him down a dry well. At first planning to kill him, finally they thought it more profitable to sell him to Arab traders for cash. Thus, Joseph was sold into slavery — and so began his lengthy trial of mistreatment.

Note that in the beginning it was not so much Joseph as his brothers who suffered the sting of parental mistreatment. Jacob heartlessly flaunted his favoritism toward Joseph. The brothers simply took the mistreatment they received from Jacob and the resentment they felt toward Jacob and laid it all upon Joseph. They tore Joseph's beautiful coat — the symbol of their father's unfairness — and dipped it in the blood of an animal. Then they took it back to Jacob with a lie about how Joseph died in the jaws of some wild animal.

Joseph, meanwhile, was taken in chains to Egypt, where he was sold to a nobleman named Potiphar. There he proved himself so valuable to his employer that he was placed in charge of the entire household. Unfortunately, Potiphar's wife also took an interest in Joseph. In fact, she used every means at her disposal to seduce him. Joseph resisted her advances, even though she tempted and pressured him day after day. Finally, unable to break the resolve and integrity of Joseph, she slandered him, accusing him of attempted rape.

Though I don't claim to have suffered anything like the intense mistreatment Joseph endured, I can identify with him and learn from him. There have been times when I have felt misunderstood, mis-judged, and falsely accused. Again and again, I've gone back to a little booklet called *Seven Secrets to Spiritual Power*, written by A. W. Tozer. One of Tozer's seven secrets is this: "Never defend your-self." Yes, we defend people who have no one else to defend them. Yes, we do what we can to clarify communication, to correct misun-derstandings. But, we will never move out of the victim role until we stop being defensive.

Healing from the hurt of slander and unjust accusation comes when we realize that because we have been justified by the work of Jesus Christ on the cross, we no longer need to justify ourselves. As Paul writes in Romans 3:24, you and I "are justified freely by His grace through the redemption that came by Christ Jesus." We do not need to defend ourselves because God is our defense.

That is one of the powerful lessons of Joseph's life: God was his defense. Yes, he endured mistreatment. Yes, he was falsely accused. And yes, he was falsely imprisoned. Yet throughout Joseph's story in the last fourteen chapters of Genesis, through the darkest moments of his trial of slavery and imprisonment, we see the words, "The Lord was with Joseph." God was present with Joseph, working out the de-tails of his story, bringing good out of all the evil that had been done to him.

While in prison, Joseph did a favor for Pharaoh's chief butler, who had been imprisoned some time before for having displeased the king. As the chief butler was about to be released, Joseph asked him to remember the favor, and to secure Joseph's own release from prison. The chief butler promised to remember — but failed to keep his promise. Joseph languished behind bars for two more years, abandoned and forgotten by his friend.

Please remember that Joseph was a flesh and blood human being like ourselves, wounded by a hurt that came not from an enemy, but from someone trusted and counted on, someone considered a friend. You may know the sting of having a friend abandon you, betray you, or break a confidence. It cuts deeply, doesn't it?

Throughout Joseph's story, we see a young man enduring trial after trial of mistreatment, seemingly every kind of injustice one could face. Yet — and this is a key lesson — *we never see Joseph surrender to the role of "victim."* I've read Joseph's story in every Bible translation I can find, and I've never found even a hint of bitterness or self-pity in his spirit. He simply refused to let mistreatment defeat him.

Joseph was thirty years old when he finally emerged from prison. From the time he was sold into slavery until his release from that Egyptian dungeon, he had endured thirteen years of injustice. But, Joseph did not merely waste away those long, painful years. He used that time to develop a winsome demeanor, a keen intellect, a godly temperament, and a spiritual gift of wisdom. When he came out of prison and was brought before Pharaoh, Pharaoh recognized these special qualities in Joseph's speech, in his bearing, in his visionary insight. So Pharaoh elevated this wise young man to the position of prime minister, second-in-charge over all Egypt.

At the end of Genesis, Joseph is reunited with his brothers. At last he has the opportunity and the power to exact his long delayed revenge against the brothers who had sold him into slavery. But Joseph doesn't want revenge. He just wants a whole relationship with his family. Joseph forgives his brothers, embraces them, and weeps over them.

As I look at this man's life and compare my own trials of mistreatment with his, I am in awe. *What a way to live!* I want to have the kind of character Joseph had. I want to see my trials of mistreatment transformed into proven character, and a positive influence on those around me.

Joseph made some right choices during some wrong experiences in his life. And I don't simply refer here to the right moral choices. His choices were therapeutically the right choices for his spiritual, emotional, mental, and physical health. He rejected resentment and bitterness. He rejected revenge. He rejected the role of a victim. So can you and I.

Donna had a home in the suburbs, and a generous income from her husband's business. She had a strong sense of belonging in her church, plus three beautiful children with a fourth one on the way. Donna felt she was living a storybook life.

Donna also had a close friend — her best friend from high school, the maid of honor at her wedding, someone with whom she could share any joy, burden, or secret. They talked together on the phone every day. They were present at the births of each other's children. So, when this friend and her husband fell upon hard financial times, Donna invited them and their children into her own home for a year so they could save money and get back on their feet.

The arrangement seemed to work well. Then just before her fourth child was born, Donna began to notice a change in her husband, Lee, and in her best friend. Though she tried to deny it, Donna suspected Lee and her friend were having an affair.

Shortly after the baby was born, Donna's life went into a tailspin. The baby came down with mononucleosis, accompanied by high fever and night-long crying. During this period of stress and sleeplessness, Lee told Donna he was leaving.

Donna's storybook world shattered. She withdrew into herself and could no longer care for the baby. She spent her days walking in circles or throwing up in the bathroom. She came to view herself as a bitter victim. Lee had her committed to the psychiatric ward of a hospital. Then he hired Donna's friend — his lover — to work in his business.

In the hospital, Donna began to gather strength and determination. She decided to fight for her marriage. In time, she was released from the hospital and returned home to care for her children. When she came home, Lee moved out. Day after day, Donna called or visited the office to confront her friend about the affair. During one of these confrontational visits to the office, Lee told Donna, "She and I are planning to get married, and we don't want you to come around here anymore."

That same week, Donna's eldest son came to her with tears in his eyes. "Momma," he said, "This just hurts too much." She hugged him, cried with him, and told him God was going to bring their family together again. Throughout the ordeal, which was to last almost three months, Donna prayed several hours each day, and sought counseling from her pastor. Her entire church upheld her in prayer.

Finally, those prayers were answered. Lee and Donna's friend broke off the relationship, and she left the office. Lee called Donna and wanted to reconcile. This was what Donna had prayed for — yet she wondered if Lee's repentance was genuine.

Their first night back together was spent at a Christian marriage seminar. As Lee listened to the speakers, read the materials, and went through the communication exercises with Donna, a realization hit him. Amazingly, throughout his affair, Lee never considered how cruelly he had hurt Donna and the children. Though he had once been a loving and considerate husband, his adulterous desire had completely shut off his sensitivity toward his family's feelings. Now, as he sat in the seminar, the shock of what he had done led him to authentic sorrow. "After everything I've done to you," he said weeping in remorse, "I can't believe you still want me as your husband." But she did want him — and she forgave him.

Several weeks later, led by God in prayer, Donna found herself ringing the doorbell of her estranged friend. The door opened and their eyes met — two women who were once best friends, yet who now stood on either side of a deep gulf of hurt. Stunned and momentarily speechless, the other woman invited her in. They talked through the night, recalling fond memories and deep hurts, expressing remorse and forgiveness. By morning, Donna's former friend was a friend again.

The story is not yet over. A marriage that has been so damaged is never mended overnight. It takes time to rebuild broken trust. Donna, Lee and their children have wounds that only counseling, prayer, and hard work can heal.

But one thing is clear: Though Donna has been to the depths of pain and betrayal, she has gradually allowed God to change her perspective from that of resentful victim to a place of healing and forgiveness, love and joy.

Chapter 17

CHOOSING JOY BY LIVING OUR LIVES AS A GREAT ADVENTURE

Years ago, a woman wrote to her pastor a letter reflecting on her life. I quote one excerpt from her message:

"Humor has done a lot to help me in my spiritual life. How else could I have raised twelve children starting at the age of 32? I married at the age of 31. I shared with some friends recently that I didn't worry about getting married in my twenties. I did leave my future to God's will. But, every night, I hung a pair of men's pants on my bed, and knelt down and prayed this prayer: 'Father in Heaven, hear my prayer and grant it if you can. I've hung a pair of trousers here, please fill them with a man.'"

Laughter is almost always one characteristic of a person whose life is marked by joy and meaning.

Someone asked Mother Teresa years ago what the job description would be for anyone who wanted to come and minister alongside her among the poorest of the poor in Calcutta. She replied, *"First, a desire to work hard because of your love for Jesus. Second, an attitude of joy."*

I live out my life with a daily commitment to two disciplines that have brought joy and meaning to my life for many years. I share them with you so that with greater intentionality we might live an even more purposeful life for Christ.

The First Discipline:
If we are to choose a life of joy and meaning, we must make our lives an act of love.

With the wildly erratic current stock market, we are hearing a great deal today in the news about investments. But as Christians, we need to always remember that the only two investments that are going to last forever are:

1. Our investment in our relationship with Christ.

2. Our investment in our relationships with people.

Accordingly, we must choose each day to make our lives an act of love as we reflect like a prism God's unconditional love to all we touch.

Our contemporary culture uses the word "love" in a wide variety of contexts. But the New Testament Greek word for "love" is a very special word: *agape*. It is different from the Greek word *phileo* (meaning love of family, brotherly love, the instinctive and beautiful love that binds family members together). It is also different from *eros* (meaning the love of attractive, beautiful, pleasing objects such as art or music, or in a similar sense, sexual love and attraction).

When Christ entered human history, He brought into the world a totally new force, the most powerful force in the world – *unconditional love*. As noted previously, when Jesus introduced this new love to His disciples, He said, "This is my commandment, that you love one another as I have loved you. Greater love has no one than this, than to lay down one's life for his friends." (John 15:12-13). This is exactly what Christ did for us.

When the New Testament was being written, the Greek language had no word for this radical new kind of love. The word agape, which occurs repeatedly in the New Testament, can only be found four times in all of the rest of classical Greek literature. The early Christians took this obscure and ill-defined word and gave it a powerful definition with their very lives: loving each other totally and unconditionally, laying down their time, their possessions, and their lives for each other.

While *phileo* love and *eros* love are based primarily on how we feel toward others (emotional), *agape* love is rooted in a decision (a choice, a commitment) we make toward others (volitional), no matter how we feel.

A mature Christian continually makes the decision to love others no matter how unlovely their actions may be toward them. If we practice this kind of love, we will find meaning and joy in our lives. And we'll find power to live a life patterned after the image of Christ. That is, after all, God's ultimate goal for each of us. Unconditional love is the most powerful force in the world.

The Second Discipline:
If we are to choose a life of joy and meaning, we must decide to live our lives as a Great Adventure.

Before his death, my friend Bruce Larson was given a grant by the Lily Foundation to research only one question: *"What are the ingredients that enable a person to become emotionally healthy?"*

Bruce interviewed pastors, psychologists, psychiatrists, physicians and specialists in many disciplines from all over the world. He then came to this conclusion:

> *"The answers to my question implied that emotional wholeness varied considerably from culture to culture. Yet, after seven years of research, I did recognize that all these experts agreed about only one particular ingredient. They said, 'a healthy person is someone who can choose risk for a worthy cause.'"*

And what greater cause in life is there than to be part of God's agenda for our time in the world? Indeed, Jesus affirmed centuries before Bruce researched this topic the reality that *"Whoever would save his life will lose it, but whoever would lose his life for the sake of Christ will find it."*

A friend of mine had just completed his annual physical at the age of 50. His physician, an outstanding Christian doctor, called my friend into his office, reviewed all his blood panels and other tests, and then said to him, "What you have is an attack of full blown middle age! Middle age is a time when people are advised to take it easy. You start to live life very cautiously. You avoid anything new or risky. And in so doing, you end up hastening the whole aging process."

Reflect with me on this: *Am I living out my life as a great adventure?*

Before her death, Mother Teresa wrote: "I used to pray that God would feed the hungry, but now I pray that He will guide me to do whatever I am supposed to do. I used to pray for answers, but now I'm praying for strength. I used to believe that prayer changes things, but now I know that first of all prayer changes us and we change things." Mother Teresa, living life as a great adventure.

Many years ago, I was seated on a platform in front of a large gathering of pastors and other Christian leaders at a national conference. As I awaited my turn to speak, I realized how deeply anxious I was, and I began to pray for peace. I will never forget how clearly I sensed the Spirit of God saying to me in that still, small voice, "Ron, the reason you're nervous is because you want to impress these people. I don't need you to impress them. I need you to love them. Ron, I don't need a grand performance, I need an act of love." That experience changed my life.

I believe with all my heart that if we begin each day asking our loving God to make our lives acts of love, and help us to live our lives as great adventures for Christ, then we will discover increasingly throughout our pilgrimages that we are living lives of joy and meaning.

Chapter 18

CHOOSING JOY BY DECIDING TO HAVE THE COURAGE TO CHANGE

Allow me to introduce you to Kay Bothwell. Kay is a sixteen-year-old student deeply admired in her public high school by Christians and non-Christians alike. Although she is merely a teenager, she has not only given her life to Christ, but she is allowing Christ to be formed in her heart. Some time ago, along with other students in her English literature class, she was given the following assignment: *"State how you would use your time if you knew that this would be the last week of your life."* Her essay reads as follows:

"Today I live. A week from today I die. If a situation such as this came to me I would probably weep. As soon as I realize that there are many things that have to be done, I would try to regain my composure. The first day of my suddenly shortened life I would use to see all of my loved ones and assure them I love them all very much. On the evening of my first day, I would, in the solace of my room, ask God to give me strength to bear the rest of my precious days and give me His hand so that I could walk with Him.

On the second day, I would awaken early in order to see the rising sun in all its beauty, which I had so often cast aside in order to gain a few more moments of coveted sleep. I would continue throughout the day to visit family and friends, telling each one, 'I love you. Thank you for the part that you have played in my life.'

On the third day, I would travel alone into the woods, allowing God's goodness and creation to surround me. I would see undoubtedly for the first time, many things I had not taken the time to notice before.

On the fourth day, I would prepare my will. The small, sentimental things I possess I would leave to my family and my friends. This being done, I would spend the rest of the day with my mother. We have always been very close, and I would especially want to assure her of my deep gratitude for her tremendous impact on my life.

On Friday, the fifth day, my life almost ended, I would spend the time with my pastor speaking to him of my relationship with Christ, and seeking advice for my final hours. I would spend the rest of the day visiting those who are ill, silently being thankful that I know no pain, and yet I know my destiny.

On Saturday, I would visit my special friend who is going through a difficult time with her broken family. I would seek to comfort her. I would be at peace now, knowing that because of Christ I am soon going to spend an eternity in Heaven. Saturday, I would spend the day with my treasured grandparents and other elderly friends, seeking their wisdom and sharing my love. Saturday night I would spend in prayer, knowing that God was by my side.

Upon waking Sunday morning, I would make all my last preparations and then, taking my Bible, I would go to church to spend my last hours in worship and praise, seeking to die gracefully, and with the hope that my life had influenced others for His glorious name. My last hour would not be spent in agony, but in the perfect harmony of my relationship with Jesus Christ."

Quite an essay! And in one of the most tragic ironies that we could imagine, it was almost one week to the day after Kay Bothwell handed in her essay, that she was ushered into Eternity. She was killed in an automobile accident just outside her home in Marion, Indiana.

This touching composition may raise some questions in our hearts. How would we spend our final days? What would we write if we were given a similar assignment? And most significantly, what are the changes that need to take place in our lives that might better enable us to prepare more fully for eternity, as we recognize the brevity and fragility of our life here on earth?

At the outset of our reflections, it may be helpful to clarify an important truth. One of the greatest misunderstandings we can live within our Christian walk is the distinction between Christ dwelling in you, and Christ being formed in you. I've heard the two phrases used interchangeably among Christians, although there is a vast distinction between the two experiences. When you received Christ, our loving God began to dwell in you. He will never leave you, or forsake you. He has come to abide with you into Eternity. But if we are not *growing* in Christ, then the character of our loving God is not being *formed* in us. Christ waits in the corridors of our hearts until we open our lives to him and earnestly state, "I yearn to change and grow so that Christ might be truly formed into the character of my life."

In the fourth chapter of Galatians, the apostle Paul gives powerful guidance to any of us who truly yearn to change, heal and discover greater joy in our lives. However, very often in our life pilgrimage because of our fear, insecurity or desire to remain in our comfort zone, we know psychologically that many of us would rather stay the way we are, even with our brokenness, character flaws or addictions, than to go through the difficult process of change that can lead to freedom, joy and significance.

Following are three examples, one from contemporary culture and two from Scripture that illustrate this sad reality:

1. Recovering patients with coronary artery disease

A recent comprehensive study following the lives of patients with coronary artery disease and fully blocked arteries revealed some sad conclusions. After having surgical procedures to save their lives, these patients were asked to make a stark and dramatic choice: *Change or Die!* Faced with the almost certain knowledge that their blocked arteries would kill them unless they made profound nutritional and lifestyle changes, 78% of these patients did not alter their daily routines *in any way!* Why is that? I'm certain there are many factors at play here. But one factor must certainly be found in the words of Elizabeth Lesser, *"How strange that the nature of life is change, yet the nature of human beings is to resist change."*

2. The Paralytic and Jesus

Picture the scene with me: A man lay by a large public pool. Helpless and paralyzed, he had been an invalid for thirty-eight years. He was one of the scores of blind or crippled people gathered around this pool because of a local legend that an angel periodically came down, stirred the water, and imparted healing power to the pool. This man was waiting, passively and self-pityingly, without hope, without expectation.

A shadow fell across the paralyzed man where he lay. He looked up, and saw that a man stood over him, piercing him with His gaze. "What do you want with me?" asked the paralyzed man.

The man eyed him levelly, "Do you want to be healed?"

At first glance, this might seem an insensitive question. Who would be so cruel as to go up to an invalid and ask, "Do you want to be healed?" But in the original language of this scripture passage, this is a much more penetrating question than that. What Jesus really asked this man was, *"Do you will to be healed? Do you choose to be healed? Are you actively committed to the process of your own healing?"* It was a question of the man's commitment to becoming whole.

I believe the reason Jesus asked this question of the paralyzed man is that He knew this man was filled with a blame mentality. When Jesus asked him, "Do you choose to be healed?" the man replied not with an answer, but with an excuse: *"No one will help me into the pool, and when I try to get in myself, someone else pushes ahead of me."* But Jesus wasn't interested in this man's excuses.

He wanted to know if the paralytic truly wanted to be healed, if he authentically had the courage to change. *"It is the nature of human beings to resist change."*

3. The Israelites and Moses – Exodus 14

After years of oppression, slavery and bondage, the Israelites were being led out of Egypt by their servant leader, Moses. But as you may remember, it does not take the children of Israel long until they want to go back to Egypt. Even though there was slavery there, even though there was bondage there, even though there was oppression there — at least they had a routine there. It was back in their comfort zone.

Moses was calling on the Israelites to live by raw faith, and to believe that one day they would arrive at the Promised Land. But many wanted to go back. *"It is the nature of human beings to resist change."*

I deeply believe that apart from surrendering our lives to God, and allowing His character to become formed into the fabric of our nature, we will not change! That abusive temper, that lack of integrity, that failure to show compassion, that profane, demeaning tongue, that inability to show deep affection to our families, that character flaw in our life will continue for years to come because: *"It is the nature of human beings to resist change."*

Throughout my adult life, I've come alongside men, women and young people who have made the difficult decision to join in partnership with God to seek to heal from an area of great brokenness in their lives. Their friends have demonstrated the courage to change. Frequently, I have guided them through a Christ-centered approach to the 12-step movement, most well-known through Alcoholics Anonymous.

Whether the struggle was with unresolved bitterness, guilt over past mistakes, alcoholism, shame, food addiction, drug abuse, anxiety, pornography addiction, low self-worth, verbal abuse or technology dependency, I have found the first two steps of Alcoholics Anonymous to be extremely helpful, when adapted to the particular area of brokenness in my friends' lives and centered in the power of Christ:

- Step One: I admitted my powerlessness over this struggle in my life.
- Step Two: I came to believe that Jesus Christ can bring healing to this area of my struggle and I surrendered my life to Him. (Adapted by Ron Lee Davis. See further, *"A Hunger for Healing: The Twelve Steps as a Classic Model for Christian Spiritual Growth"* by J. Keith Miller, and *"Healing Life's Hurts"* by Ron Lee Davis.)

Walking through these first two steps on a weekly basis with so many has convinced me of the effectiveness of this approach for those who have the courage to change.

How will I know that Christ is not only *dwelling* in me, but that His character is being *formed* in me?

The Apostle Paul anticipates that question and answers it in Galatians 5:22-23: "For the *evidence* of the Holy Spirit invading our life will be love, joy, peace, patience, kindness, goodness, faithfulness, gentleness, self-control, against such as these, there is no law." How will we know if Christ is being formed in us? We seek discernment from God, and from those who know us best: Do both our living Lord, and our dearest loved ones sense that, in a growing way, the evidence of love, joy, peace, patience, kindness, goodness, faithfulness, gentleness and self-control mark our lives?

As we mature in our walk with Christ, we are to become absolutely clear in our understanding of this Biblical Principle: *The central mark of our becoming more like Christ is discovered by a growing evidence of the nine Fruit of the Spirit in our lives.*

Put another way, the life where Christ not only *dwells*, but where Christ is being *formed* is the Spirit-filled life. Further, we understand that it is not a matter of our saying to ourselves, "I'm going to *try* with all my might to be more loving, more joyful, more peacefully...." Rather, it is a matter of saying from our hearts, *"I fully yield, I totally surrender, I completely capitulate my life to Christ, asking Him in partnership with my submissive will to invade my heart so that the nine Fruit of the Spirit would be demonstrated more fully in my life for the Glory of God."*

Methodist Missionary to the poor, E. Stanley Jones, burnt out and exhausted in his ministry, knelt down in a primitive hut in India, and poured out his heart to God. He prayed passionately, *"Lord, Jesus, I will strive for you no more! Come and live Your life through me!"* Those who knew E. Stanley Jones best said that from that day forward he lived like a man whose life had been transformed. So may his prayer be ours today: *"Lord Jesus, I will strive for you no more! Come and live your life through me!"* For it is only in this act of the surrender of our wills to Him that we be empowered to have the courage to change, and to allow the Fruit of the Spirit of joy to become more evident in our lives.

Chapter 19

CHOOSING JOY AS WE WIN OVER WORRY

Paul Baker lived his life in the fast lane. He was the classic Type-A driver. His life was marked by anxiety until an event took place which began to change his perspective and allowed him to begin a pilgrimage whereby he would eventually win over worry. He writes of his journey in this letter:

"One evening I came home to be greeted by a tall, teen-age girl whom I had never met. My son, David, had struck up a conversation with her in the grocery store and invited her to stay in our home. Her name was Debbie. Her parents had beaten her and kicked her out of their home. She was battered physically and emotionally. She lived with us for five weeks, recovered, and now lives with an aunt. My son David took time for the moment, and it made such a difference.

On another occasion, I scolded David several times for not being home on time in the late afternoons. He said nothing in his defense for his repeated behavior. Only much later did I discover where he had been and what he had been doing. One of his friends had an eye disease and was gradually going blind. David was reading books to his friend. My son took time for the moment.

One Friday afternoon about 3:45, David took time for the moment. He took just a moment to call me on the phone. We visited for a while and decided to go shopping; we planned a shopping trip to buy his mother's Christmas present. We agreed to meet at 6:00 p.m. As we ended the conversation on the telephone that day David said to me, 'I love you, Dad. Goodbye.' Fourteen minutes later David died in an automobile accident.

How precious that brief moment on the telephone has become to me now. How many fathers never hear those words 'I love you'? How many of us are too busy to take time for the moment? David's concern for the moment has caused me to care more, look deeper, search harder, pray longer, and finally — to come to some sense of balance and peace in my life."

David Baker left a legacy of taking time for the moment. In these stressful days in which we live, what legacy will *we* leave?

In Matthew 6:25-34, Jesus uses the same word five times. Translated into English, that word is *worry*. It is a Greek term coming from two Greek words: *merizo* meaning *divided*, and *nous* meaning *mind*. Biblically, to worry means to have a divided mind.

Most of us can identify with this definition. We all know what it's like to be interacting with our friends when deep in the midst of the conversation our mind is partly there with them, and partly focused on some worry regarding a distant yesterday or some future concern. We have a divided mind.

So Jesus says in the greatest sermon ever preached in Matthew 6:

Verse: 25: *"Do not worry about your life."*
Verse 27: *"Which of you by worrying can add one day to your life?"*
Verse 28: *"Why worry about your clothing?"*
Verse 31: *"Therefore, do not worry!"*
Verse 34: *"Do not worry about tomorrow."*

The late columnist Erma Bombeck gave us wise counsel regarding worry:

"If I had my life to live over again, I would have waxed less, and listened more. Instead of wishing away nine months of pregnancy and complaining about the shadows over my feet, I would have cherished every minute

of it, and realized that the wonderment growing inside of me was my one chance in life to assist God in a miracle. I would never have insisted the car windows be rolled up on a summer day because my hair had just been teased and sprayed. I would have invited friends over for dinner, even if the carpet was stained and the sofa was faded. I would have eaten popcorn in the good living room, and worried less about the dirt when you lit the fireplace. I would have taken time to listen to my grandfather ramble on about his youth. I would have burnt the pink candle sculptured like a rose before it melted while being stored in the garage. I would sit cross-legged on the lawn with my children and never worried about grass stains. I would have cried and laughed less while watching television, and more while watching life. And when my child kissed me impetuously, I would never have said, 'later, later! Now go get washed up for dinner!' There would have been more, 'I love you's', more, 'I'm listening', more 'I'm sorry's. But mostly, given another shot at life, I would seize every minute of it, look at it, really see it, try it out and never give that minute back until there was nothing left."

What keeps some of us from living life this way? The Scripture calls it living with a divided mind: *worry*.

Three life principles have guided me in my pilgrimage as I seek to win over worry:

1. **Deliberately stop being absorbed with an endless obsession for the material things of this life which do not last.**

A number of years ago, I had the privilege to speak at a conference with a man named "Charlie Life-is-Tremendous Jones". Some of you may be familiar with Charlie Jones, who was a gifted motivational speaker and committed Christian before his death in 2008.

Charlie told a story that day at the conference about a time when he was living with his family in their home in Florida. A flood tore through their community one day in the aftermath of a fierce rainstorm, with four feet of mud seeping into the basement of Charlie's home. Charlie had recently refinished and remodeled his basement, transforming it into a beautiful den, a study area, and his ornately decorated office. As the four feet of mud crept into his study, the sludge covered all his files where Charlie had organized his motivational talks, his legal documents, his speaking schedule – it even covered his brand new desk. As the dirt and water crept up the walls, it destroyed all of his plaques, diplomas, and awards. As Charlie 'Life is Tremendous' Jones walked down the steps into the basement and plodded through the mud, he wasn't feeling too tremendous. He said he felt discouraged. But then he said it was as though God spoke to him and said, "Charlie, don't worry about these things. I was going to burn them all up one day anyway."

Like some of you, I've lost many material things through the years that I once held dear. As I've scaled down my life, with every loss I can testify that God keeps reminding me what's *really* important to hold on to.

2. Intentionally start living your life for those things that are Eternal.

What are the things that are Eternal? I think many of us know there are two: *our relationship with God and our relationship with people*. Everything else – just like Charlie's basement – will one day be destroyed. But our relationship with God and our relationships with people will live on forever. So it behooves all of us to humble our hearts before God in prayer and offer to Him words something like this:

> *"Heavenly Father, I commit on this day that from here on out, I will invest my life in my relationship with You and my relationship in people – because everything else will pass away."*

3. Consistently begin to take time for leisure.

Make certain that one aspect of that leisure is spending time with God and with people because everything else will pass away.

On the last evening of every month, I climb into bed and review a series of questions I wrote years ago that have guided me as I seek to win over worry, and live a life of joy and gratitude.

Why not join me today in reflecting on your answers to these ten questions about this past month?

1. Did I consistently model a lifestyle of joy with my family and friends?
2. Did I intentionally create some positive memories with my loved ones?
3. Did I say, "I love you" a lot to my family and friends?
4. Did I have a daily time of study, prayer and meditation?
5. Did I frequently enjoy the beauty of God's Creation in nature?
6. Did I exercise consistently and eat in a nutritious way?
7. Did I find ways to invest my life in the next generation?
8. Did I take a Sabbath day (a day of rest and renewal) every week?
9. Did I read good, quality books rather than just surf the internet?
10. Did I seek out opportunities to serve others in need?

While your set of questions may differ from mine, these types of questions can lead us to a deeper sense of inner peace and joy as we seek to win over worry.

Chapter 20

CHOOSING JOY WHEN LONELINESS STRIKES

A friend of mine, a widow spent thirty years married to one man. One day her loving Christian husband suddenly succumbed to a heart attack. That was several years ago, and ever since then her life has been a succession of lonely, joyless days.

"You have no idea what it's like," she said, "to come home every day, to fix a meal for one, to set the table for one, to wash the dishes for one, and to look across the table night after night at the chair once occupied by my husband. When someone tells me time will heal it all, I get angry! Time hasn't healed my pain."

I want to share with you an excerpt from a letter I received some time ago. The letter was written by a young woman who had been deeply in love with a man with whom she was engaged to marry. Suddenly he had broken their engagement and left her for another. Now she was leaving her church and community, and going back to her home town to live with her parents. *"I can't stay here anymore,"* she wrote, *"Neither a good job nor a friendly church can remove the long, lonely ache from my heart. I'm going back home now more lonely than I ever dreamed possible."*

An active Christian layman came to know loneliness intimately and tragically. Over a period of time, he gradually lost his health, then his job, then his wife, and finally he lost the greatest joy of his life — he lost his little son in a tragic accident.

In his grief, all he had to turn to were his photo albums. One day he took the photos of his son and covered one huge wall of his house, ceiling to floor, with them. And that evening his took his own life.

In my book *Gold in the Making: Where Is God When Bad Things Happen to You?,* I attempt to build a strong case for the reality that the Apostle Paul very likely battled deep seasons of loneliness. In this chapter, I want to list four specific actions Paul took when this unwelcomed guest approached his life. I believe these four guidelines will serve us well as we seek to lovingly encourage others to choose joy when they are feeling lonely and isolated:

1. When battling loneliness, Paul sought the companionship of his friends.

Paul took the initiative to reach out to cherished loved ones like Timothy, Luke and Titus. When we feel the tendrils of loneliness start to close in around our hearts, we need to take the initiative toward fellowship with wisely chosen, loving friends — whether we feel like doing this or not. The tree of loneliness is fed by the stream of isolation.

Years ago, the California State Department of Mental Health studied 7,000 adults from ages 30 to 59. One of the dynamics under investigation in this study was the correlation between friendship and health. The researchers found that people without long-term friendships have from two to five times the normal mortality rate for their age group, and experienced higher than normal incidences of cancer, heart disease, circulatory disease, and other ailments.

In Genesis 2:18, God said *"It is not good for man to be alone."* Nowhere is this more true than when we or one of our loved ones battles loneliness.

2. When battling loneliness, Paul continues to serve others.

The Apostle understood until the very end of his life that only a cause greater than himself could ever truly rid him of his loneliness.

A war correspondent during World War II was traveling through a war zone. At the site where he was staying one night, there was a nurse who some time ago had been widowed. The nurse was caring for a soldier whose leg had been ripped to shreds in the battlefield that day. There was bone and blood and muscle – and a terrible stench in this primitive little clinic.

All this suffering was repulsive to the war correspondent. He leaned over to his journalistic colleague as he watched the nurse care for the wounded soldier, and whispered, "I wouldn't do that for a million dollars."

He didn't intend for this widowed nurse to hear the comment, but she did hear his words. Tenderly, she looked at him and quietly said, "Neither would I. Neither would I."

In essence, the nurse was saying, "I'm not doing this for money. I'm doing this for Christ." There is great therapeutic value when facing the loss of a loved one, as this widow had experienced, as with any other form of loneliness — to choose to serve others.

3. When battling loneliness, Paul remembered to care for his spiritual, mental and physical needs.

It's well documented that when people are battling loneliness, they often tend to let themselves go. They tend to stop eating in a nutritious way. They tend to stop reading the Bible or other inspirational books. They tend to stop exercising. They often tend to not get enough sleep.

Paul models a different response. There is a deeply touching passage tucked away in II Timothy 4: Paul is near the end of his life now. He's lonely, and in his loneliness, he calls for his beloved friend, Timothy to come to him before winter as he lives out his final days in a prison cell. He asks Timothy to bring three items with him: his cloak, as the dampness of the dungeons turns to winter cold; his books, so that he can read and study; and his scriptures, what we would today call the old Testament. Paul, in a lonely season of his life, knows he needs to take care of his physical, spiritual and cognitive health. So do we. So do our loved ones.

4. When battling loneliness, Paul chose to stay close to Christ.

I was twenty-one years old, hitchhiking across the beautiful Welsh countryside on a holiday from my studies at the University of

London. My journey alternated between high exhilaration and deep loneliness. I sometimes reflected on all the miles that separated me from my family and friends in Iowa, and I often felt out of touch with God. Near the close of one day, feeling very homesick, I sat down on one of the green Welsh hillsides, shrugged off my backpack and began to read from Psalm 139.

Where can I go from you Spirit?
Where can I flee from your presence?
If I go up to the heavens, you are there;
If I make my bed in the depths, you are there.
If I rise on the wings of the dawn,
If I settle on the far side of the sea,
Even there your hand will guide me,
Your right hand will hold me fast.

As I was reading these words, I felt a quiet assurance wash over me: God Himself was with me. Though I was halfway around the world from home, He was beside me —and I no longer felt so lonely.

The human heart is afflicted with a longing, a homesickness that is so deep and so vast that only something much larger than ourselves can fill it. My old friend Lloyd Ogilvie wrote these words shortly before his death, "Loneliness is none other than homesickness for God. Intimate communion with Him is our home."

All our human relationships, as important as they are, are *horizontal* relationships. Our relationship with God is of a different dimension: it is *vertical*. God reaches down to us in our loneliness and lifts us up toward a joyful communion with Him. The wonderful paradox God offers us is that in order to escape the prison of our loneliness, we must learn the discipline of solitude. Intimacy with God is our home, and no matter where we are, He is never far from us. God is far greater than all the longings of our hearts, and when we lose ourselves in the love and wonder of His presence, we have true freedom from loneliness.

Chapter 21

CHOOSING JOY THROUGH A LIFE OF SERVANTHOOD

Many years ago, there was a young physician who lived in Southern California. This man was a gifted surgeon who was often referred to as "The Doctor to the Stars" due to the celebrities who were his patients. This physician experienced a dramatic encounter with Christ, and as he began to grow spiritually, he asked in prayer daily, "How can I best use the skills you've given me for the furtherance of Your Kingdom?" Gradually, he began to sense that God was calling him to become a medical missionary.

At the appropriate time, the young doctor told his non-Christian partner of his plan to leave their practice and register in a Missions School. His physician friend responded to the news by exclaiming, "You're a foolish man to throw away a lucrative practice here in Los Angeles and go off to the middle of nowhere!"

The Christian surgeon continued his plan, received his Bible and missionary training degree and accepted his first assignment. It was to a primitive country, a poverty-stricken land, an illness plagued village.

The medical missionary had been in the village six months when his non-Christian partner, in the midst of an overseas vacation trip, decided to fly in and see his friend. The day his old colleague was to arrive in the simple little town, the missionary was preparing to perform a complicated surgery on a middle-aged woman.

The physician's old partner asked in a scoffing manner, "Do you remember how much money you would have made for just this one surgery back in California?"

The medical missionary responded softly, "Oh, yes. I remember. I would have made a lot of money." With a taunting demeanor, the partner then asked, "What will you make for it here?"

The Christian doctor responded gently, "Well, I'll receive several things. First, if you look closely at this woman's hand, you'll notice that her fist is clenched. If you could open up that fist, you would see that she has a couple of coins she wants to give our mission. Second, if you glance into the next room, you'll see several small children. They are her children, and if she lives, I'll receive their thanks and love. And you know, there is one more thing I believe I'll receive...."

Skeptically, his old colleague asked, "what could that be?"

The Christian missionary replied tenderly, "One 'well done thou good and faithful servant' from my Lord Jesus Christ."

Philippians 2:6-7 tells us that Jesus Christ did not think equality with the Father was a thing to be grasped, but rather that he humbled himself and took on the form of a *servant.*

As I study scripture, it becomes increasingly apparent to me that the central goal for the Christian is to seek to become more like Christ (see Philippians 3:10, Colossians 1:27, Romans 8:28-29). If the goal of our lives is to become like Christ, then it is imperative that we understand what Christ is truly like. While there are many places in scripture where we are told by *others* what Christ is like, there is only one place in all the Bible where Christ himself tells us what he is like. Jesus says in Matthew 11:28, *"I am gentle and humble in heart."*

Gentle. Humble.

Unfortunately, both of these terms have suffered through the centuries. They have often been ill-defined. Their definitions have been corrupted. We can become confused in the process.

According to the New Testament, the word, *gentle* means *strength under control.* The word "humble" means "to stoop low as to *serve.*" Whenever we ask, "When am I most like Christ?" the answer will be: "When I choose to be a servant."

Years ago, there was a caretaker leading a group of English tourists through the home of Ludwig van Beethoven. This was the home where Beethoven lived in the final years of his life, and where he composed his greatest works. There was one rather brash, arrogant English woman on this particular tour. As the group made its way through the home, she couldn't wait to come to the room where Beethoven's piano could be found.

Finally, the group walked through the various corridors and rooms and stairs of Beethoven's home until they reached the room containing the Master's piano. The caretaker carefully walked over to the piano and gently removed the cover over the instrument. The tour guide then stated to the group, "This is the piano where Beethoven composed his greatest works."

Upon hearing these words, the brazen English woman pushed her way through the crowd and sat down to begin to fumble and bumble her way through one of Beethoven's sonatas. When she had completed the musical piece, she turned to the caretaker and said, "I suppose many of the tourists who come here play on Beethoven's piano."

The caretaker gently responded, "Well, last year the great pianist and composer Ignacy Paderewski was here on his tour, and many in the crowd urged him to play, but Paderewski's response was, "Oh, no. I am not worthy. I am not worthy."

On the night that our Lord was betrayed, there were plenty of disciples who felt they were worthy. They came to The Last Supper in arrogance, not humility. They came in pride, not servanthood. So, Christ realized that one final time — one last time — He would have to model to them what the life style of a Christian is to be like.

We read this account in John 13. In other parallel passages in Scripture, we discover the reality that on the night before the cross, everyone was willing to fight over the throne, but no one was willing to fight over the towel.

You may remember from Matthew 20 that James and John and the others had joined in an argument over who would sit at the left and right hand of Christ. So Jesus, in the midst of the meal, girded himself with a towel, and began to quietly wash each disciple's feet.

Servanthood Principle #1: Servanthood will be unannounced.

If we vulnerably look back over our lives, at times perhaps all of us have performed acts of service in hopes of gaining recognition or credit. Yet, when we study the life of Christ, we observe that our Lord continually confronted the scribes and pharisees for the verbal, visible way that they used to *announce* their servanthood. The Servanthood of Jesus will be unannounced.

Shortly before his death, my father, a kind and humble pastor, was asked to write a brief biography of his life and ministry. He concluded his autobiography with his favorite poem, which he modeled every day to me – and to so many others:

"I do not ask that crowds may throng the temple
That standing room be priced
I only ask that as I voice the message
They may see Christ.

I do not ask for churchly pomp or pageant
Or music such as wealth alone can buy
I only ask that as I voice the message
Christ may be nigh

I do not ask that men may sound my praises
Or headlines spread my name abroad
I only pray that as I voice the message
Hearts may find God.

I do not ask for earthly place or laurel
Or of this world's distinctions any part
I only ask that when I have voiced the message
That I may find my Savior's heart

I'm often convicted when I read the prayer of Ruth Harmes Calkin:

"You know, Lord, how I serve you with great emotional fervor – in the limelight. You know how I effervesce when I promote a fellowship group. You know, Lord, my genuine enthusiasm at a Bible Study. But, how would I react, I wonder, if you pointed to a basin of water and asked me to wash the calloused feet of a bent and wrinkled old woman. Day after day, month after month. In a room where nobody saw and nobody knew."

Servanthood Principle #2: Servanthood will not be selective.

We read in John 13:5 "Jesus washed *their* feet." Have you ever stopped to reflect upon who the "their" included? It includes Judas. Read the flow of Greek text. Gain the historical setting. The "their" includes Judas! The "their" includes the one who is about to betray Christ.

That's the portrait I've been waiting for some gifted Christian painter to sketch in for us: Jesus humbly kneeling down and washing the feet of the one he *knows* will betray him.

Servanthood will not be selective!

Years ago, I wrote out a simple sentence that I had framed and set on my desk to read frequently: *"Look past the irritation to the need."* I would often ask God to help me, when a difficult person came into my life, praying, *"Loving God, help me to look past the irritation to the need. What brokenness is in the person's life that causes him to act the way he does? Remind me, Heavenly Father, that so often the person I am least naturally drawn to is perhaps the one who most needs my love right now."*

Many years ago, an old friend of mine and national Christian leader, chose to honor this second servanthood principle. I'll call my friend "Rob". One night Rob's wife, Sandy was home alone. Rob was away on a business trip. Their children were spending the night with friends. That night Sandy heard a knock on the door. She asked who it was, and a man answered that his car broke down, that he needed to use the phone. Sandy let him in.

Instead of moving toward the phone, he advanced toward her, telling her he intended to rape her. She began to fight him off, and finally broke loose, lunging out the front door of their home. Screaming for help, she ran onto the front lawn. The man followed, cursing. He whipped out a gun, leveled it at Sandy, and pulled the trigger several times. Sandy fell, shot twice in the back. She crawled agonizingly to the street and collapsed as the neighbors began to come out of their homes, startled by the gunfire. Someone called an ambulance, and she was soon rushed to the hospital.

The man got away.

Within an hour, scores of people around the country were praying for Sandy as she struggled for her life. Her doctors didn't give her a good chance to live, and if she lived, they said, she would probably never walk again.

Today she is alive and able to walk. It's a beautiful miracle of healing. But, there's yet another miracle of healing to this story.

I was talking to Rob one day many months after this happened. Rob began to tell me what had happened to the man who shot his wife. He was captured, tried, convicted, and sentenced to prison. During the process of that trial, God did a miracle of healing in the hearts of my friends, Rob and Sandy. After this man was committed to prison, Rob and Sandy went there, and visited a number of times with this man. They shared Christ with him. Today, the ex-convict is an active Christian layman in his church.

As we continue in this moving passage, observe what a masterful teacher Jesus is. Those of you who have a background in educational methodology will immediately observe the magnificent teaching model Jesus now provides. Notice how after Jesus has washed the disciples feet, he asks them a penetrating question. Many of you who have been teachers know that's a great pattern to follow. You do something, and then you ask a question. Jesus has just done something. He has washed his disciples' feet. Now he asks this crucial question: *"Do you know what I have done for you?"*

After Jesus lets them wrestle with this question for a few minutes, he gives his disciples and us – one final Servanthood Principle. In John 13:14, Jesus says, *"If I have washed your feet, you ought to wash..."* Now pause with me and reflect logically: what should he say? Many would guess, "If I have washed your feet, you ought to wash my feet." That's just good logic, isn't it? That's just our culture, isn't it? That's just the law of reciprocity we've all been taught, isn't it? I scratch your back, you scratch my back. If I wash your feet, you wash my feet.

But that's *not* what Jesus said. It would have been so much easier if Our Lord had said, "If I wash your feet, you ought to wash my feet" — because we would love to wash the feet of Christ. Instead, Jesus says something so much harder, and now the cost of discipleship is so much greater on our lives. Because he says, *"Because I have washed your feet, now you have got to wash one another's feet.' — even that person who is so hard to love."*

Servanthood Principle #3: Servanthood involves serving others, not just Christ.

Serving Christ can be the greatest joy in life! Serving others can be extremely demanding work! One component of that work is to take the time to discover the deepest needs of our loved ones. Perhaps everyone would say that we all want to be servants to our families. Yet, scripture teaches us that we cannot truly be a servant to our loved ones until we identify the needs of our loved ones. As a part of my morning quiet time, I ask God daily, *"Help me to understand how I can best be a servant to my son, my daughter, my grandchildren, my other loved ones by taking the time to understand their greatest needs, heartaches and struggles."* We cannot truly be effective servants without a deep identification with each family member and other loved ones.

Identification! You know who did this better than anyone else in human history? Jesus Christ – who left the splendor of Eternity to become one of us. He reached out and touched us, and wept with us, and shared His life with us, and identified with our every struggle. Therefore, we are not surprised to read in Hebrews 4:15 these words:

> *"We do not have a high priest who cannot identify with us, but rather we have an advocate with the Father who understands our needs and has been tempted in every way as we have been, yet without sin."*

Christ identifies with us so that we might truly *identify* with those we seek to serve.

Al Quie is a man who identified with a friend he yearned to serve. During the time I lived in Minneapolis, Al Quie served as a U.S. Congressman for the State of Minnesota. Al Quie reached out as a servant to Chuck Colson, when he had been disgraced as Special Counsel to President Richard Nixon. As you may recall, Colson was imprisoned for his part in the Watergate scandal and in brokenness, had surrendered his life to Christ. When many in churches around the country were skeptical about the validity of Colson's conversion, Al Quie reached out to him with love and compassion.

Chuck Colson was serving time in a minimum security prison, he received word that his son was addicted to drugs, and that because of this crisis, his family was fragmented and broken. Al Quie reached out to his new Christian brother, visited him in prison and on one occasion said to him, "Chuck, I've studied my law books carefully, and I've discovered this rare status written over 100 years ago that states that for the type of crime you've committed and for the length of time you have already served, another man can come and serve the remainder of the term for you. I want to do that for you, Chuck. You need to be with your family."

And Chuck Colson began to weep. Deeply moved, visibly shaken by this offer, Colson said, "I don't understand why you would do this for me." Al Quie said, "It's because of John 13. When Jesus washed his disciple's feet, he told us to wash one another's feet, to live a life of a servant, and then he said, 'By this shall all men know that you are my disciples, that you love one another." Colson graciously refused to allow his new friend to take his place, but motivated by this act of servant love, spent the rest of his life ministering to men and women in prisons.

Near the end of his life, medical missionary Albert Schweitzer wrote, "I don't know what your destiny will be, but one thing I know: the only ones among you who will truly discover joy are those who will have sought and found how to serve."

Servanthood involves joyfully serving others, not just Christ – because we understand as Christians that *"whatsoever you do for the least of these,"* you do for Christ as well (Matthew 25:40).

Chapter 22

CHOOSING JOY THROUGH LIVING A LIFE OF UNCONDITIONAL LOVE

It was Christmas time when a little boy named Moss Hart and his father decided they would travel by subway to downtown New York City to shop at a large discount department store. Their objective was to find one Christmas present for little Moss Hart. Moss' father was a poor man. He worked hard, but he toiled in a factory where the weekly wages he received were very small.

Moss knew exactly what he wanted for Christmas. He wanted either a miniature chemistry set or a beginner's printing press. His loving father had much less expensive gifts in mind. Up and down the aisles of the huge department store they walked. After a long time had passed, Moss would find a toy that he liked. His father would then ask the store salesman, "How much would this toy cost?" Upon hearing the price, the father would gently shake his head and quietly respond, "I don't think this is what we had in mind."

Then, as the father and son walked a bit further along in the store, the father would find a less expensive toy and show it to his boy. As much as Moss tried to pretend he liked the toy, he really didn't want it. His discerning father could recognize his son's disappointment, and he would place the toy back silently.

This process continued until Moss and his father reached the very last aisle, and still there was no Christmas present. The father and son left the store empty handed.

Years later, Moss would reflect upon this experience: "I heard my father jingle some coins in his pocket and I knew it all in a flash. Dad had pulled together about 75 cents to buy me a Christmas present, but he had not dared say so in case there was nothing to be had for so small a sum. As I looked at him, I saw a look of despair and disappointment in his eyes that brought me closer to him than I had ever been before in my life. I wanted to throw my arms around him and say, 'It doesn't matter, Daddy. It doesn't matter. I understand. Just being with you is better than any old printing press. I love you,

Daddy. I love you.' But instead, we just stood there shivering beside each other other for a moment, and then we started silently back home. I didn't even take his hand on the way home, nor did he take mine. We were not on that basis. Nor did I ever tell him how close I felt to him on that night – that for a little while the concrete wall between father and son crumbled away, and I knew that we were just two lonely people struggling to reach each other."

What is it about those of us who are fathers? Call it pride. Call it cultural training. Call it macho reserve. But sometimes many fathers, even against the true yearning of their hearts, create an invisible wall that causes a separation between themselves and their families. As Moss Hart put it: "two lonely people struggling to reach each other – but we were not on that basis."

Yet, I would affirm from Scripture that we human beings were *made* to be on that basis — to be in loving, vulnerable, expressive, transparent, authentic, affectionate relationships with one another.

Gary Crosby, eldest son of the Bing Crosby family, understood the moat-like distance that can separate a father from his family. Gary had a father who attained a great deal of success in the world's eyes as a singer and actor. Yet, he writes these words about his dad:

> *My father was an excellent communicator professionally, but found himself totally unable to express love for his own children. He could not express joy and affirmation in any words that we could even understand. Because of his inability to communicate love, our entire family suffered terribly."*

Perhaps some of you can relate to the words of Moss Hart and Gary Crosby as you reflect back on your own family of origin. And as you consider that reality, you know you desperately do not want to reproduce that distance with your own Loved Ones.

We have author John Powell to thank for putting into simple terms five levels of communication that can guide all of us as fathers, mothers and family members as we seek to show more deeply our love for one another.

He writes, *"There are five levels of communication and very few of us ever reach level five with our loved ones."*

Level One: Clichés. Clichés like, "How's it going?" "What's up?" "Have a good day!" Every culture has clichés, and it is very seldom that they have significant meaning attached to them.

Level Two: Facts and Reports. For example, "I saw the film *'The Lion King'* with my grandson Griffin" or "The Vikings play the Bears Sunday."

Level Three: Opinions and Convictions: For example, reactions and beliefs: "I liked the film *'The Lion King'*. It touched my heart." "When Rachael and I had dinner together, the food was delicious, but the service was poor." Powell argues convincingly from research that most families rarely move beyond Levels one, two and three in their communication with one another for any significant amount of time.

Level Four: Feelings. These are expressions of emotions where the masks are taken off and vulnerable truths are articulated. Often, tears may even be shed. At this level, a college age daughter may share, "It's so good to be home for the summer mom, but I'm feeling anxious about going back to school this fall. The pressure academically and socially and morally is so great. I'm feeling afraid." In 2017, when we were evacuated due to the Thomas Fire in Santa Barbara, I had a chance to genuinely share with my granddaughter, Caitlin: *"I really miss being at our home with you, but I've loved the times* *we've had together this week. I've so enjoyed our talks and I'll miss you when we each go to our homes."*

Level Five: Maximum Truth Shared with Maximum Love. Powell argues that this is the finest form of communication for the Christian. Unfortunately, this is too often the rarest form of communication for the Christian. It takes a deep level of spiritual and emotional maturity to traffic in Level Five, for it is here we see the expression of genuine confession of sin, authentic forgiveness, and heartfelt healing — and unconditional love.

Here at Level Five, we share our deepest dreams. We share our most painful tears. We share our embraces openly with one another. At its' root is the heart of the Christian life in action. Its' basis is Ephesians 4:15, where we are told we are to grow up in every way unto Him who is our Head, unto Christ, as we learn to speak the truth in love. This Biblical Truth is what gives a purpose to our Level Five sharing of feelings. Here we don't just share random feelings. Here there is a purpose behind our vulnerable sharing: It is to build up one another in Christ.

For example, recently I was driving my granddaughter, Caitlin, home from soccer practice and we began to discuss how important our friends are to our lives. I shared, "Caitlin, you have always had such wonderful friends. I believe one reason for this is that you always take such a genuine interest in your friends' lives — and in mine. My life is so enriched by your friendship."

As we seek to communicate at the deepest levels with our families, I offer three final principles to guide us in this great endeavor:

1. **We are loving unconditionally when we model consistently in the home what we say we believe in our church and community.**
   The sunlight slanted over the Rockies, painting the trees, the ground, and the houses with a warm golden glow. My brother Paul

and I were jogging on the running trails that wound among the hills west of Denver, near the Red rocks Ampitheatre. I remember the scene clearly: the dirt paths beaten down by the shoes of many other runners, the hilly and wooded countryside, the stands of brush where the deer would pause and stare in amazement as these strange human creatures loped by.

Paul and I ran this ten-mile course every evening during our stay with his family. It was a good time to be alone with my brother. We took the course at an easy pace, and we talked as we ran. We talked about a lot of things, but mostly reminisced about the days when we were growing up together in Iowa; about the good times we had; about our mom and dad; about our faith in Christ.

"Ron," Paul said as we pounded down a gently sloping grade, "you and I are both following Christ. There are so many wrong turns we could have taken in our lives. A lot of choices, a lot of temptations. But we're still following Jesus — just like Mom and Dad used to pray we would when we were kids. Why do you think that is?"

I thought about it for a few strides. Then I responded, "from a human perspective, I'd have to say it's the way Mom and Dad lived."

"They lived what they said they believed," I continued. "The things Dad preached in the pulpit, the things they both taught us at home, the times they disciplined us — it all matched up with the way they lived."

"Right," said Paul, huffing slightly as we started up a hill. "I thought that's what you'd say. Integrity. Walking your talk. When kids see that in their parents, they want to live that way, too. Dad was the finest man I ever knew. He always lived what he believed. I want to be that kind of dad to my boys."

Paul was that kind of dad.

If there was one lesson I learned from my 10-year stint as a Youth Pastor in a wonderful, large Minneapolis church, it was that nothing drives young people away from Christ more quickly than a lack of congruency between what their parents say they believe and the way they live at home.

2. **We are loving unconditionally when we trust in the truth that God is working when and where we cannot be working.**

So often through the years, parents would come into my office exasperated that one of their children, often during the adolescent years, was far away from God. Perhaps the teenager or young adult child was experiencing a season of doubt or rebellion. Often during our conversation, I would gently plead with the parents, "Don't count the score at half time. The game is not over yet. We are in this process with our children through all Eternity with God." And so often, in God's timing, the child would "come home."

In my favorite parable, often referred to as The Parable of the Prodigal Son — the father in this story doesn't go chasing after his boy who is in a season of defiance.

Rather, he trusts that in God's way and in God's timing, God will do something he, the earthly father, cannot do: change his boy. Perhaps some of us will need to trust in the same way as we place our sons and daughters in God's loving hands.

3. **We are loving unconditionally when we refuse to allow our stress to harm our loved one's security.**

Years ago, Psychologist David Elkind wrote a classic book entitled The Hurried Child. In the book he writes, "When we parents are under stress, we need shortcuts. We need to get things done quickly. So we don't take the time to deal carefully and in depth with our children. Parents under stress tend to see their children in the shorthand of symbols rather than the often hard to decipher long hand of personhood."

Examples:

Symbol – My son is an athlete

Symbol – My daughter is an A student

Symbol – My son is a computer whiz…

… Rather than: "My son has a sensitive, melancholy temperament. He is very tender toward the less popular students in his class. He can be prone to mild depression and can appear to become anxious when feeling overwhelmed." That's the long hand of personhood.

Out in the world, our loved ones will tend to be labeled by the shorthand of symbols. The home needs to be a haven where our loved ones are treated with the long hand of personhood.

When we take the time to consistently model in the home what we say we believe, to trust that God is working where we cannot be working with our loved ones and to refuse to allow our stress to harm our families' security, we will be well on our way to leaving a legacy of love and joy.

Chapter 23

CHOOSING JOY IN THE MIDST OF LIFE'S GREATEST LOSSES

The Jaeger family's cabin cruiser rose and fell on the surface of the Atlantic Ocean. It had been a good family day for George Jaeger, his three sons, and his father. Despite the strong, brisk breeze and the gathering clouds, the day had been mild and the sea friendly.

Toward evening, however, the wind grew stronger, and the sea rose ominously. George Jaeger knew how to read the warning signs of the sea. With respect for the power of the elements, but without fear, he nosed his small craft toward home. Suddenly, the boat's engine sputtered, died, and refused to start.

The storm grew angrier. The sky darkened, and the waves rose to heights of ten feet and more, pounding over the sides and swamping the boat. A relaxing boat trip had rapidly become a thing of horror.

George Jaeger calmly, efficiently, tied a rope through the laces of the life jackets, tying himself, his father, and his sons together. As their small boat broke apart and sank beneath the crashing waves, the Jaeger men and boys bravely committed themselves to the Atlantic Ocean.

Together they struggled, straining to stay alive, but losing strength and hope. First one son, then a second, then a third drowned. Finally Grandpa Jaeger, weary from the struggle and choking on the sea water, gave up the fight and disappeared beneath the waves.

Eight hours later, George Jaeger staggered ashore alone, pulling the rope which still was attached to his three sons and his father, all dead.

Months after surviving this horror at sea, George Jaeger was able to say, "My youngest son Cliff was the first to go. I had always taught our children not to fear death, because it meant being with Christ. Cliff was a little boy, and he fought and fought the waves. The last thing he said to me was, 'Dad, I'd rather be with Jesus than to go on fighting anymore.' He died quietly with courage and dignity."

On that stormy day, George Jaeger and his wife faced an incredible avalanche of loss. Losses enter our lives in a wide range of ways. To set the stage for this chapter, allow me to briefly categorize the types of losses we often encounter through the seasons of our lives.

1. *The Loss of a Loved One.*

   For you that may mean a spouse, a parent, a child, a sibling, a friend. I want to broaden this first category by suggesting there is a sense of loss we face in life when we are separated from those we love not only by death, but also by distance. You may have a child, a family member, a beloved friend who is far away from you now, and in that reality there is a sense of loss.

2. *The loss of a dream, a goal, a great plan for the future you held deeply in your heart.*

   Today you know that dream will never be realized, and in that realization, there is a sense of loss.

3. *The loss of your health or the health of a loved one.*

4. *The loss of your marriage.*

   Your spouse has perhaps left you for another, or passed away.

5. *The loss of your youth.*

   This is the realization that we are perhaps approaching the final season of our lives, and for some of us that reality brings a great sense of loss.

Very probably, each of us has felt — or is currently feeling — a sense of loss in one way or more of the categories listed above. My goal in this chapter is to help us gain God's perspective on life's greatest losses, and in so doing, to discover a life of deeper joy.

I have observed throughout my life two common reactions to loss. First, there is The Natural Reaction. Our natural reaction may be a multiplicity of emotions such as anger, shock, bitterness, fear, panic, depression, denial, grieving and remorse. We must understand these feelings are natural and normal, and ought not be judged by anyone.

In his classic book, *Lament for a Son*, Nicholas Wolterstorff writes as he grieves over the death of his son.

> *"There's a hole in the world now. In the place where he was, there's now just nothing. A center, like no other, of memory and hope and knowledge and affection which once inhabited this earth is gone. Only a gap remains. A perspective on this world has been rubbed out. Only a void is left. There's nobody now who saw just what he saw, knows what he knew, remembers what he remembered, loves what he loved. A person, an irreplaceable person, is gone. Never again will anyone apprehend the world quite the way he did. Never again will anyone inhabit the world the way he did. Questions I have can never now get answers. The world is emptier. My son is gone. Only a hole remains, a void, a gap, never to be filled."*

The second reaction is The Divine Reaction. This second reaction *does not cancel* out the first reaction. Rather, it *fulfills* the first reaction. This second reaction *does not nullify* the first reaction. Rather, it *completes* the first reaction. The Divine Reaction, after a period of shock, denial, anger, grief and depression, begins to say, "I accept this loss. I will never be the same again. I may not understand this loss, but I will submit to it. Even though it is deeply painful, I see it now as a part of the reality of life and before you, oh, loving God. I will grow closer to you through this profound loss."

Deep suffering and heartache remain within the heart of the

Christian when loss invades like an unwanted guest. But the Apostle Paul gives us the balance between these two reactions when he writes, *"We sorrow* (that's The Natural Reaction), *but not as those who have no hope"* (that's The Divine Reaction) (I Thessalonians 4:13). It is not the *absence* of sorrow. It is the absence of *hopeless* sorrow.

George Mattheson faced a long list of losses in his life. He had lost his sight, his friends, his family, and the love of the only woman he ever cared for. All his plans and dreams for the future were dashed. And it was in the depths of this terrible loss that Matheson sat down at his desk, and wrote the lines of a beautiful hymn I grew up singing, as perhaps did many of you, about the One Love we can always turn to, who can restore joy even in the midst of excruciating pain.

O Love that will not let me go,
I rest my weary soul in Thee;
I give Thee back the life I owe,
That in Thine ocean depths its flow
May richer, fuller be.

Through my affiliation with *The Fellowship of Christian Athletes*, I developed a friendship with a man named Brian Sternberg. In 1963, Brian was named The Outstanding Athlete of the Year by *Sports Illustrated*. At that time, he was the World Record Holder in the pole vault. One day, he was working out on a trampoline, and landed in an awkward position, injuring his spine in such a way that paralyzed him from the neck down. He remained paralyzed throughout the rest of his life until his death in 2013 at the age of 70.

I have watched hundreds of high school young men and women be moved to tears as Brian Sternberg, sitting there in his wheelchair, talked about his love for God, and about his losses. Brian Sternberg lost his health, he lost his ability to walk, he lost much of his weight, and even the experience of going through one day without constant pain. I asked Brian, "What's your life verse?" and he told me, "My life verse is Philippians 3:7-8, '*For whatever was to my gain I now consider loss for the sake of Christ. What is more, I consider everything a loss compared to the surpassing greatness of knowing Christ, for whose sake I have lost all things.*'"

Brian Sternberg, like Nicholas Wolterstorff, George Jaeger, and George Mattheson — and hopefully you and me — all learning, to gain God's perspective on life's greatest losses. For it is our loving God alone who can establish joy in our hearts during seasons of painful loss.

Chapter 24

CHOOSING JOY THROUGH THE SEASONS OF LIFE

Jesus said to Peter, *"When you were younger, you girded yourself and walked where you wished; but when you are old, you will stretch out your hands, and another will gird you and carry you where you do not wish."* *This He spoke, signifying by what death he would glorify God. And when He had spoken this, He said to him, "Follow Me." Then Peter, turning around, saw the disciple whom Jesus loved (John) following, who also had leaned on His breast at the supper, and said, "Lord, who is the one who betrays You?" Peter, seeing John, said to Jesus, "But Lord, what about this man?" Jesus said to him, "If I will that he remain till I come, what is that to You? You follow Me." Then this saying went out among the brethren that this disciple would not die. Yet Jesus did not say to him that he would not die, but, "If I will that he remain till I come, what is that to you?*

John 21:18-23

He was 17 years old. She was 16. They met each other, and quickly fell in love. Three months later, they were married. Three babies later, a multitude of resentment and animosity later, she left him. Judy had become disillusioned with Bill's complete preoccupation with his career. Coupled with this struggle was Bill's indifference toward working at their relationship. Periodically, Judy would call from some unknown destination to ask how the children were progressing in school. Each time she called her estranged husband, Bill would always ask, "Where are you? Please come home!" Each time, Judy refused.

Finally, after a long season of struggle and prayer, Bill realized how much he truly loved Judy, and how poorly he had treated her.

Now, more than anything else on earth, Bill yearned for reconciliation with his wife.

Bill hired a detective, and paid him a large sum of money, asking him to search throughout the United States to find his wife. After several months, the detective found Judy in a rundown hotel in Des Moines, Iowa. Bill immediately caught the next flight out of his west coast city, and flew to Des Moines.

His hand quivered as he knocked on the door of the hotel room where Judy was living. As she opened the door a bit, she saw her husband, and instantly began to weep. The tears were tears of joy. She said to Bill, "I'm so glad you've come. I had prayed for so long that you would come." The husband was ecstatic by her response, and gently asked, "Well then, honey, why didn't you come home?" Judy replied, "Many times you have told me you loved me *from afar.* Many times when you were off building your client base or preoccupied with your work in some distant city, you would call me from some hotel room to tell me you loved me. But now I know you love me, *because you cared enough to come.*"

This love story with a happy ending because Bill cared enough to come. There is another love story with a joyful ending about a Man who cared enough to come. He cared enough to come to earth. He cared enough to come to a rugged cross. He cared enough to come to an open grave, and He did not call out from a long distance away to say, "I love you." Rather, *He cared enough to come!* It is the greatest love story in human history, and as we turn to the New Testament, we find four accounts of this love story, which is the life, teaching, ministry, death and resurrection of Jesus Christ. The first three accounts of the life of Christ, Matthew, Mark and Luke are written by three men who wrote their Gospels at approximately the same time. These three accounts have a similar emphasis, and are therefore sometimes called the *Parallel Gospels,* or *Synoptic Gospels.*

But then, there emerged this fourth account, and it was written by a man who knew the heartbeat of Jesus Christ as did no one else during our Lord's earthly ministry. This man delayed fifty years, and then near the end of his life, empowered by our loving God, he wrote a completely *unique* account of the life of Christ, written through the lens of a man who was the best friend of Jesus. His name: The Disciple John, also known as the Beloved Disciple. The Gospel of John is at once the most simple, and the most profound love story in human history.

It is a distinctive Gospel, and in John 21, we once again see its uniqueness, for here we find a conversation between Christ and Peter that is found nowhere else in the Bible. Further, in this remarkable dialogue, we find three life principles that have been life transforming for me, and for many Christians who are seeking to live their lives with joy.

Jesus begins the conversation by saying to Peter, *"'Truly, I say to you Peter, when you were young, you girded yourself and walked wherever you wanted to go, but when you are old, you will stretch out your hands and another will gird you and carry you to where you do not wish to go.' This Jesus said to show by what death Peter was to glorify God."* John 21:18

Through the centuries, Bible students have wondered what Jesus was truly communicating in these surprising words to Peter. In the final chapters of the Gospel of John, Peter looms large: his vacillating personality, his bold affirmations ("Thou Art the Christ"), his cold denials ("I don't know the man!"), his three responses to the three questions of Jesus, "Peter do you love me?"

In his Gospel, John tells us a great deal about Peter. But one thing John doesn't tell us about Peter is the details surrounding his death. The historian Eusebius does. In the third volume of his Ecclesiastical History books, he tells us Peter was in Rome in 61 AD during the reign of Nero, who was slaughtering Christians. Peter yearned to escape, but sensed that God was calling him to "stand firm and remain in Rome." So he did, and he was arrested, and imprisoned along with his wife. One cold morning, he was taken with his wife to a place of execution. Peter was forced to watch as his wife was violently tortured, and prepared for her death. As the preparation took place, Peter said only three words to his wife: "Remember the Lord." Then she was executed.

The next morning arrived and Peter was led to his place of execution. It was to be for Peter an execution from a cross. Peter's first words as he approached the cross were simply, "I am not worthy to even die in the manner of my Lord." So the soldiers took the cross, and pounded the nails into the hands and feet of Peter, and then Peter, upon his only request, was crucified upside down.

Now we see more clearly what Jesus was saying when he told Peter, *"When you get older, Peter, you are going to be led to a place you do not want to go, and they are going to stretch out your arms in a way you don't want them stretched out — and your life will be taken from you."*

In John 21:18-19, Jesus tells Peter something about his past, and something about his future. Christ says in essence, *"Peter, in your past, the way things used to be, you would walk wherever you wanted to walk."* It is a picture of a self-reliant, confident, assertive man. And that's Peter, and that could be many of us. That's Peter's past.

But then Jesus says in essence, *"Now that my call to discipleship is upon your life, your future is going to be far different than your past. You're not going to be able to live your life the way you want to live it. It's going to be taken from you. You're not going to be able to walk wherever you want to walk. Your oppressors will lead you down a path where you don't want to go, and you're not going to be able to stretch your arms in whatever way you want. They will be stretched out for you on a cross. You will die in brutal fashion as a martyr."*

Three life principles emerge from this powerful passage.

1. Our present life-style is no guarantee for the same kind of future. Don't postpone.

The reality of this uncertainty must motivate us as Christians to not postpone the building of an authentic character that will enable us to live with joy in all the unknown tomorrows of our lives.

Several years ago in a span of three months, eight long-time friends of mine passed away, including my life long family friend Ed Nordland. Most of the eight friends were younger than me. Most died suddenly.

As I wrote several eulogies in that brief season of my life, I was reminded that present lifestyle is no guarantee of the same kind of future for any of us. God is continually teaching me that we must leave room for the uncertain parentheses that will inevitably come into our lives. We had better leave room for the unexpected rebellion of one of our family members. We had better leave room for the potential of failure in our careers. We had better leave room for illness to strike us or one of our loved ones. We had better leave room for the separation or divorce of one of our cherished friends. We had better leave room for God leading us to a place we may not want to go, as He did with Peter in John 21.

This deeply moving passage continually reminds me that we need to be preparing now with the disciplines of prayer, study and loving fellowship with other Christians to build character into our lives. Then, when a trial comes upon us like an unwelcome guest, we will be prepared to face it with the help of a loving God. *Present life-style is no guarantee for the same kind of future. Don't postpone.*

Jesus gives us a second vital life principle beginning in John 21:20. *"Peter turned and saw following them the disciple whom Jesus loved."* Picture the scene with me. Jesus and Peter are engaged in the most personal, impactful and important discussion about the future life of Peter that Peter is ever going to have! But Peter notices in the background some footsteps. *"Oh, there's John"*, Peter observes. And in the midst of this deeply profound discussion between Jesus and Peter, Peter asks, *"Well, but what about John?"* In John 21:22, Jesus lovingly confronts Peter and says, *"If it is my will that John remains until I come again, what is that to you? Peter, you keep following me."*

All of us can fall into the comparison game. We can, in our own nature, want to know about somebody else. Jesus says to us, "Never mind about My will for him right now. You be concerned about your own walk with Me." This leads us to our second vital life principle.

2. Personal obedience is an individual matter. Don't compare.

Generally, in our Christian pilgrimages we're either *maturing* or *comparing*. It's very difficult to do both at the same time. When it comes to decisions in life that are not specifically addressed in scripture, we live out our obedience in different ways. We make different choices about the various ministries where we are going to serve, and give of ourselves sacrificially. We make different choices about whether we are going to drink socially. We make different choices about how we will disburse the financial blessings God gives us. We make different choices about what movies we will watch. And, in all these areas, and so many more, Christ says to us, like he says to Peter, "I'll tell you your story, not his. Be more concerned about *maturing* than *comparing*."

Years ago, a well-meaning Christian came to me deeply concerned because he had just seen a married couple in our church going into an "R" rated movie at a multiplex theater. A few evenings later, I was having dinner with this couple when they mentioned to me how much they had been inspired by watching the film, *"Glory"* earlier that week. As you may recall, *"Glory"* is a civil war drama starring

Denzel Washington and Morgan Freeman, which contains a storyline with a strong Christian message of redemption. The film was rated "R" because of violence.

We live out our obedience in different ways. In Jeremiah 29:13, God says to us, *"You will seek me and find me when you seek me with all your heart."* We cannot be seeking God with our whole heart, and at the same time be comparing ourselves with a judgmental spirit to everyone else.

As we see from their conversation, Peter is trying to switch his dialogue with Jesus over to John because Peter wants to make certain everything is *fair*! Perhaps every one of us has fallen into a *fairness mentality* at times. In response to Peter's obsession with fairness, Jesus responds by saying, in essence, "The future for you, Peter holds the reality that you are going to watch your wife be executed. You are going to die a violent martyr's death. John is going to live to a ripe old age in meditation and reflection. Then he is going to write a Gospel that will be the most beloved Gospel in the history of the world. That doesn't make one of you better than the other. We live out our obedience in different ways." *Personal obedience is an individual matter. Don't compare.* Few things rob us of a life of joy more than comparing ourselves to others.

Notice what happens next in this amazing dialogue. In John 21:23 we read, *"The saying spread abroad among the brethren that John was not to die, yet Jesus did not say to him that he was not going to die, but only: 'If it is my will that he remains until I come, what is that to you?'*

Do we recognize what is happening here? Perhaps the same reality happened to you this week. The message was garbled. People muddled and distorted what Jesus said. Rumor started and gossip began to spread.

Jesus said in essence, *"Peter, if John remains until I come again, what difference does that make to you?"* and probably by the next morning someone was saying, *"Hey, did you hear that Jesus said to Peter that John gets to live here on earth until Jesus returns?!"* This leads us to our final vital life principle:

3. **People will often misunderstand what Christ is leading you to do. Don't worry.**

People misunderstood Jesus sometimes. People will misunderstand men and women who follow Jesus sometimes. If we have gone before God with a pure heart, if we have studied and prayed humbly, if we have sought out Godly Christian counsel, and then come to a place where we can say from our hearts, "This is what I believe God is leading me to do, and I know it's going to be misunderstood, and I may even be criticized for it", then we can with confidence go ahead and act upon what Christ is calling us to do, because above all else, we want to honor Him with our lives.

Dietrich Bonhoeffer, writing from a prison cell shortly before his execution, penned these words: *"When Christ calls a man, he bids him to come and die."* Bonhoeffer was right. It may not be a martyrdom like Bonhoeffer, Peter, Jim Elliot, the apostle Paul — but Jesus is requiring of us the subordination, the surrender, the capitulation of our wills, our plans, our future to Him — that He might take our lives, which we have yielded to Him, and begin to allow God to shape and mold us into the image of Christ.

Many people misunderstood a decision my old friend Bill McCartney made years ago. As some of you recall, Bill McCartney was the head Football Coach of the Colorado Buffalos from 1982 – 1994. When Bill was coaching at The University of Colorado, there was an outstanding quarterback on his team named Sal Aunese. After a spring workout one afternoon, Sal Aunese began to experience severe pain in his stomach. Thinking perhaps it was the flu, Sal went to see his doctor. It was not the flu. It was cancer.

Aunese's cancer rapidly spread into his lungs. This tragic news was shared with Sal in March. In April, Bill and Linda McCartney's daughter Kristy gave birth to a boy named Timmy. The father of this precious little baby was Sal Aunese, who had been, by his own admission, sexually active with many women on campus.

Question: If you were Bill McCartney, how would you feel? I've known long time active church members who would have disowned their daughters in situations similar to this one, as well as held only contempt for Aunese.

Not Bill McCartney. Humbly going before God, and not fearing the reaction of other people, Bill reached out in unconditional love to his daughter Kristy, to his new grandson, Timmy and to Sal Aunese.

By this time, Sal had been hospitalized. Bill McCartney visited him daily. On one particular visit, Bill tenderly shared the Gospel message with Sal, and Aunese received Christ into his heart.

Bill wrote these words to me several months later, "God has truly blessed our daughter Kristy and Sal with a perfect, beautiful, healthy child, and then, just five short months after Timmy's birth, with all of us by his side, our Lord called Sal home. Sal's valiant battle with cancer is over, and Sal now lives in Eternity with Christ."

There was one more letter enclosed in the envelope Bill sent to me. It was a letter written by Sal Aunese to his teammates just days before he died. He wrote, in part, these words:

> *"Don't be saddened that you no longer see me in the flesh, because I assure you I will always be with you in Spirit. Trust in the Lord with all your heart. I now see because of Bill McCartney's testimony that this is the only way. Hold me dearly in your hearts, as you know I do all of you. I love you, Sal."*

May we all in our lives be sensitive to God's compassion and love, as Coach Bill McCartney was — and may we always remember as we seek to live a life of joy:

Present lifestyle is no guarantee for the same kind of future.
Don't postpone.

Personal obedience is an individual matter.
Don't compare.

People will often misunderstand what Christ is leading you to do.
Don't worry.

Chapter 25

CHOOSING JOY AS WE RESTORE THE WOUNDED

In his challenging book, *Love, Acceptance and Forgiveness*, Pastor Jerry Cook tells of an angry phone call he received from the pastor of a nearby church. This pastor was upset because some of the members of his own church were leaving to go to the church where Jerry Cook pastored. Cook knew that this man needed to get it off his chest, so he let him speak his mind.

In the course of the conversation, this pastor hinted that the people who were moving from his church to Cook's church were only those who were so broken, so beaten down by life, or by some personal tragedy such as divorce or alcohol abuse, that they couldn't really contribute much to the life of a church anyway.

"You know what you are out there?" he finally asked of Jerry Cook. "You're nothing but a bunch of garbage collectors."

Cook mentioned this conversation in church one Sunday, and a man came up to him after the service. He was the man who owned the local garbage collection company, and his face was positively glowing.

"Let me tell you something about garbage," he said. "There's a landfill near here. For ten years we used it as a place to dump trash and garbage. Do you know what's there now? A beautiful park."

Cook concludes, "I've seen garbage in a person's life become beautiful, too. I've seen the stench of brokenness turned into the fragrance of heaven. That's our business. We can't worry about what critics think or say. Where is God going to send the 'garbage' for recycling if He can't put it on our doorstep?"

How about you and me? When a loved one stumbles in some area of his life, do we walk toward them or away from them? So often I'm reminded of the haunting words of Henry Drummond when he asks, *"How many prodigals are kept out of the Kingdom of God by the unlovely characteristics of those who profess to be on the inside?"*

One of my favorite stories is about a little boy who would pass by a pet shop on his way home from school. Every day he would stop at that pet store and play with the dozen or so puppies that were kept in a pen in the display window. Finally, he got up enough courage to ask the owner of the pet shop how much one of the puppies would cost. The owner of the shop told him the price, and the boy went home and began saving his weekly allowance.

He returned a few weeks later with his piggy bank tucked under his arm. Smiling broadly, he lifted his bank onto the counter and broke it open. "It's all there!" he said joyfully.

"So I see!" said the owner, as he began to sort through the nickels, dimes, and quarters on his counter. "There's the pen. Pick out any puppy you like."

The puppies were yelping, wagging their tails, and crawling all over reach other — all but one who sat forlornly in one corner of the pen. The boy reached past all the other puppies, picking up the one lonely puppy in the corner. He brought it to the counter and presented it to the shop owner.

"Oh, you don't want that one," said the man.

"Why not?" asked the boy.

"Well, he's crippled. Just look at his leg. Son, you want a puppy who can run and play with you in the park. You don't want a crippled puppy."

The little boy set the puppy down on the floor and lifted the cuffs of his pants, revealing a set of braces, reminders of a crippled childhood disease of a few years before. "Yes, he's crippled. But I'm crippled, too. I thought since we're both crippled, we could be better friends."

We're all crippled, aren't we? Our wounds come in many different forms, but we're all crippled.

When we can acknowledge our own areas of brokenness, we begin to become much more loving and compassionate toward the wounds of others.

A few years ago, a friend of mine, in a moment of great confusion, committed an act so heinous that he was sent to prison. All who knew Ted (not his real name) were shocked by his crime, and many of his friends walked away from him.

My friend Dave Barry chose to walk in the opposite direction. He reached out to Ted, listened to him on his lonely nights as he awaited trial, stood by him at the sentencing phase of the legal procedures, visited him regularly in prison, helped him get reconnected back into society upon his release, and guided him into a spiritual renewal of his faith. On occasion, I would travel with Dave to the prison and would always be deeply touched by the genuine sorrow, remorse and repentance that marked Ted's life. Today, Ted is leading a faithful Christian life in large measure because one man decided to love a friend who had stumbled badly.

Years ago, a friend of mine in another city fell into a life of moral failure. In the aftermath of his mistake, he felt ostracized by his church. I called him on the phone to encourage him and ask how he was holding up in the midst of overt rejection. He said, "You know, Ron, I felt like I was out in the ocean drowning, and everyone in my congregation was standing on the beach, pointing at me, judging me. But one friend in my town just loved me. It felt like he swam into the cold ocean waves and put his arm around me and saved me." Today, my friend's life is restored and whole through the love of his friend.

Will we be more like the friend who swam out to save this man or more like the folks pointing and judging on the beach the next time someone we know stumbles and falls?

Authentic joy is a wonderful by-product given to us by our gracious God when we play a part in restoring our wounded loved ones, and watch them discover wholeness and forgiveness, to live lives of meaning and gratitude.

Chapter 26

CHOOSING JOY THROUGH THE POWER OF ENCOURAGEMENT

The gifted violinist Niccoló Paganini was standing before a packed house in Italy surrounded by a full orchestra. Paganini began to play one of his favorite selections, which was an extremely difficult concerto. Shortly after he was underway in the playing of this composition, one of the strings on his violin snapped. Suddenly beads of perspiration began to grow on Paganini's forehead. He frowned for a moment, but he continued to play his beloved instrument, improvising beautifully. To his amazement, shortly thereafter a second string broke — and then a few moments later, a third.

Now there were three limp strings dangling from Paganini's violin as the Master performer continued to improvise and complete the difficult composition on the one remaining string.

Immediately, the audience stood to their feet and applauded! After a time, in the midst of this standing ovation, the crowd began to cry out, "Encore! Encore!" In that moment, Paganini now faced another *attitude choice*. He could, in frustration and disappointment, refuse to come back and play an encore with only one string remaining on his violin. Or he could *choose an attitude* of courage and risk, and attempt to play an additional selection using his masterful instrument with only one string intact.

Paganini turned to the crowd, and with a twinkle in his eye, smiled and then placed the single-string Stradivarius beneath his chin. He played a beautiful encore selection as the crowd whispered in amazement, "Paganini and one string. Paganini and one string." I would add "Paganini and one string — and an *attitude choice*."

Like Paganini, you might believe that in some arena of your life, you feel like you're down to one string. And now you have an attitude choice to make: to give up or courageously go on.

The Apostle Paul writes in Philippians 2:5: *"Your attitude should be the same as that of Christ Jesus."* Notice with me that Paul proceeds this statement with four "ifs" — and they *all* have to do with *attitude*.

1. "If there is any encouragement in Christ."
2. "If there is any incentive in love."
3. "If there is any participation in the Spirit."
4. "If there is any affection and sympathy." (Philippians 2:1)

And then Paul says: *"Complete my joy by being of the same attitude"* (Philippians 2:1). Please notice that the very first ingredient that Paul gives to us in his attitude checklist is: The attitude of encouragement. One component of living our daily lives with a Christ-like attitude is to intentionally offer encouragement to those God brings into our path.

After my brother's death at the age of 41, a friend from a distant city called me to ask if he could fly in the next day to see me. While I welcomed his visit, I also wondered, "Is something wrong? Have I hurt him in some way? Is he going through a personal crisis?"

The next day my friend arrived and we spent several hours together. He asked how I was holding up in my grief. At one point, he said simply, "Ron, I just flew in for no other reason than to seek to encourage you." Our hours together were filled with affirmation, compassion, tears and love. I wept openly as I said goodbye to my friend later that day. Driving home, I reflected on how deeply moved I was by this man and his encouragement that day.

Perhaps you don't have to have the funds to fly to another city to encourage a friend. For many years, I've made an annual goal of writing at least ten messages of encouragement each day — either via email, Facebook, or with pen and paper. I know you may do much more than that simple commitment, but I have found it helpful to set specific encouragement goals. *"Your attitude should be the same as Christ Jesus, "* Paul writes. And one component of living our daily lives with a Christ-like attitude is to intentionally offer encouragement to all our loved ones.

Perhaps there's no other group of people in all the world who need encouragement more than children. Our precious little ones are formulating opinions about themselves and developing a vision regarding who they can become.

The biographer of Benjamin West, the great 18th century artist, writes about the attitude choice of encouragement made by West's mother toward her children. He writes, "One day Benjamin's mother went out for groceries, leaving Benjamin in charge of his little sister, Sally. In his mother's absence, Benjamin discovered some bottles of colored ink and began to paint a portrait of Sally. In doing so, he made a considerable mess of things with ink blots all over the kitchen. His mother returned home, saw the mess, but said nothing. She picked up the piece of paper and saw the drawing. "Why!", she exclaimed, "It's Sally! It's Sally!" Then she stooped down and kissed little Benjamin. Throughout his life, Benjamin West would regularly say: "My mother's kiss that day made me a painter." Psychological research is teaching us that a single interaction with a person can often change the entire direction of a life. So often, that single interaction needs to be one of encouragement.

The Apostle Paul, in Philippians 2, understood the power of choosing an attitude of encouragement. So did Randy Goodrum, who wrote the lyrics to one of my favorite songs. Recorded by the Christian artist Anne Murray in 1978, the lyrics read:

"You held my hand when it was cold
When I was lost you took me home
You gave me hope when I was at the end
And turned my lies back into truth again
You even called me friend.

I cried a tear, you wiped it dry
I was confused, you cleared my mind

I sold my soul, you brought it back for me
You held me up, and gave me dignity
Somehow you needed me.

You gave me strength to stand alone again
To face the world out on my own again
You put me high upon a pedestal
So high that I could almost see Eternity
You needed me. You needed me."

(You Needed Me, Performed by Anne Murray, written by Randy Goodrum)

The Apostle Paul is saying to us in essence in the opening verses of Philippians 2, "I want you to take a long look at your short life, and to participate with an open, non-defensive heart in an attitude check. I want you to candidly reflect on these questions:

1. Do I live my life daily with an attitude of encouragement?
2. Am I seeking daily the empowerment of God to make my life an Act of Love?
3. Do those who know me best fully realize how much I care for them, believe in them and yearn to encourage them?"

In Philippians 2:5, *"Your attitude should be the same as Christ Jesus."* This powerful statement naturally raises the question in our hearts, "What exactly was the attitude of Christ Jesus?" Paul immediately answers our question in verse 6-11, in one of the most magnificent passages in all of the New Testament. In a word, Paul tells us the attitude of Christ Jesus was the attitude of a *servant*. Read with me the single most precise statement of the person and work of Christ given to us in the whole of Scripture:

> *"Jesus Christ, though He was in the form of God, did*
> *not think equality with the Father was a thing to be*

*grasped, but he emptied Himself, taking on the form of a **servant**, being born in the likeness of men. And being found in human form, he humbled himself and became obedient unto death, even death on a cross."*

Two principles emerge from this beautiful passage today:

1. **A primary way that we can measure our spiritual growth is to ask ourselves,** *"Am I modeling an Eternal attitude of encouragement to others in the midst of the daily challenges of life?"*

We now know that when we honor this first principle of application, there are specific benefits for our own health and well-being. Research from The Harvard School of Public Health clearly verifies that when a person lives with a genuine attitude of encouragement and gratitude, the risk of both heart disease and hardening of the carotid artery walls drops dramatically. Our own longevity and health span can be increased when we transform a self-absorbed attitude to one of encouragement and service to others.

2. **A primary way that we can measure our Spiritual Growth is to ask ourselves** *"Would those who know me best say that I am consistently living my life with a Christ-like lifestyle of servanthood?"*

"You held me up and gave me dignity." I particularly love that line from the Anne Murray song. Daws Trotman was a man like that — always holding somebody up. The founder of *The Navigators*, an international ministry that helped to shape my life as a young man, Daws poured his life into scores of young people and encouraged them in Christ.

One day, Daws Trotman was in a boat on a lake with some of his family members and friends. The boat swerved unexpectantly and three people — Daws Trotman and two women — fell into the rough waters. Daws Trotman could swim, the women could not. So he swam to them, and finally reached the first woman, brought her back to the boat, and held her up until someone was able to grab her. Then he swam toward the second woman and brought her back to the boat using all the strength he had left to hold her up until someone was able to pull the second woman to safety. By now Daws Trotman, in a state of total fatigue, went under the choppy waves and drowned.

A few years ago, I ran up the hillsides of Glen Eyrie Christian Conference Center in Colorado to find the simple gravestone that read: *"Daws Trotman — 'Greater love hath no man than this, that he lays down his life for his friends.'"* (John 15:13)

Billy Graham came to preach at the Memorial Service for Daws Trotman. The week that Billy preached at the funeral, there was a photo of Daws Trotman in Time Magazine. Someone had captured a picture of him holding one of the women up to the boat just before he drowned. The caption read: *"Daws Trotman — Always Holding Somebody Up."*

What caption could be put under our picture? Could it authentically be *"Always Holding Somebody Up"*?

Chapter 27

CHOOSING JOY AS WE OVERCOME FEELINGS OF INADEQUACY

The following was a letter written by the wife of a pastor as she openly shares her feelings of inadequacy:

"My husband and I have often felt on the edge of an ill-defined despair in our ministry together. During these difficult times, we have felt a variety of things: a desire to either quit or run, a temptation to fight back at some-one, a sense of being used, manipulated or exploited, and above all, a deep awareness of our inadequacy."

Haven't we all, at times, felt like the pastor's wife? A desire to quit. Wanting to run. A yearning to fight back. Feeling manipulated, used, exploited and above all, a deep awareness of our own inadequacy.

Examples of feelings of inadequacy are many and varied:
- The feeling of inadequacy with being unable to provide for our family, spiritually, emotionally and/or financially.
- The feeling of inadequacy in the areas of just getting up in the morning with any sense of enthusiasm, energy and vitality. Some of us may feel increasingly burned out, worn out, fatigued and depressed. Accompanying all those emotions is a deep-seated feeling of inadequacy.
- The feeling of inadequacy that comes in the midst of a deteriorating marriage. Your partner is pulling away, and you are not sure how to respond — and in that uncertainty you feel completely inadequate.
- The feeling of inadequacy related to illness, a chronic medical condition, or an approaching surgery. You are feeling anxious and you wonder if you have the courage and strength to face what lies ahead — and in that uncertainty, you feel inadequate.
- The feeling of inadequacy related to an addiction in our lives — alcohol, drugs, work, exercise, pornography, food, verbal abuse — and in our failure to overcome the addictions, we feel inadequate.

- The feeling of inadequacy that can accompany the reality of knowing you are a divorced person, and that your marriage has failed.

I'm defining inadequacy in this way: *"to be insufficient, to be incapable of performing or achieving, to be unable to accomplish a certain objective, to be deficient in dealing with a situation in life."* And perhaps if there are any words in all the New Testament with which many of us can identify with the Apostle Paul, it would be found in II Corinthians 2:16 where Paul has just described all of the attributes and characteristics that are expected of a Christian leader. Having sketched in all of these qualities, he asks, "Who is *adequate* to do such things? Who is *adequate* to be that kind of person?" And my response throughout my life has been "Not me!"

I have struggled since childhood with feelings of inadequacy. Often these emotions have robbed me of a life of joy and gratitude. Through the seasons of my life, I have battled feelings of inadequacy as a student, an athlete, an author, a husband, a father, a grandfather, a friend, as a man, and as a Christian.

In the midst of this struggle, three great truths from scripture have given me hope and encouragement. I pray these Biblical principles will hearten and inspire you today in your life journey:

1. **Acknowledging our inadequacies is a crucial step to becoming empowered by Jesus Christ and His Love.**

One of the prayers I offer each morning before the sun rises is that when I interact with others today, they will sense such an aroma of love, compassion and kindness exuding from me that those who cross my path will sense that I am filled with the very Spirit of God. However, there is a challenge for me in this prayer. Simply stated, the challenge is that I can't be filled until I am emptied. Scripture teaches us that we can't be fully empowered with the Spirit of God in our lives until we begin to rid ourselves of our self-reliance, self-sufficiency, and desire to be viewed as self-made men and women. God yearns for us to come to Him vulnerably admitting our brokenness.

When Harriet Beecher Stowe wrote Uncle Tom's Cabin in 1852, over 300,000 copies of the book were sold in the United States, a number of sales that was unheard of at that time in our history. And then, after 300,000 copies were sold in the U.S., the book was translated into over a dozen different languages. Leo Tolstoy described Uncle Tom's Cabin as one of the greatest achievements in the history of humanity. As you probably know, Uncle Tom's Cabin did more than any other book in its' time to bring about the freedom of slaves in our country.

Yet, when Harriet Beecher Stowe was interviewed regarding the impact of the book she authored, she always, with great sincerity, responded in the same way: *"I? The author of Uncle Tom's Cabin? Oh, no! The Lord wrote it. I was just an instrument in His hands. To Him alone goes all the glory."*

Whenever I read these words of Harriet Beecher Stowe, they remind me of some lyrics that would be written 75 years after her death. I used to sing these words when I was part of a singing group called *The Children of Hope* many years ago:

"Just let me live my life
Let it be pleasing, Lord, to Thee
And if I gain any praise Let it go to Calvary
To God Be the Glory, To God Be the Glory, To God Be the Glory
For the things He has done."
~ Andre Crouche, *My Tribute*

As I have noted previously, if there is one truth that so many of my friends in the 12-step movement such as Alcoholics Anonymous have encouraged me to understand, it is that authentic healing from broken parts of our lives cannot begin until we acknowledge that we are powerless in ourselves to overcome our addictions, struggles, compulsive sins and battles with inadequacy.

If there is one principle that is consistent throughout all of scripture, it is that men and women who have been used in a great way for God all have one characteristic in common? These men and women all came to a point where they authentically acknowledged their own inadequacy — and at that point, God filled them with His Spirit, and then these people were used to transform their culture.

Admitting our own inadequacies and surrendering our lives to Christ is the crucial first step to becoming filled with God's Spirit and finding our adequacy in Him.

2. Seeing Ourselves as God Sees Us is a Crucial Step to Overcoming our Feelings of Inadequacy.

At the heart of our beings, many of us face an identity crisis because we do not know who we are in God. And because we do not experience in our hearts who we are in God, we feel inadequate. Out of our feelings of inadequacy and insecurity, we can begin to play all sorts of psychological power games in a misguided attempt to achieve a healthy sense of self-worth.

- The Biblical Christian believes in his heart, and teaches his loved ones that we are wildly, extravagantly, relentlessly, unconditionally loved by God.
- The Biblical Christian believes in his heart, and teaches His loved ones that we are *"fearfully and wonderfully made"* (Psalm 139:14) in the very image of God with unique gifts and talents.
- The Biblical Christian believes and teaches His loved ones that when Jesus, The Good Shepherd, reaches out for His sheep to hold them in His gentle arms, He reaches out for us.
- The Biblical Christian believes in his heart, and teaches his loved ones that in the midst of a superficial culture that is trying at every turn to teach us that our worth is based upon our position, or title, or affluence, or appearance, that if we are stripped away of everything, we have tremendous worth because we know who we are in the sight of God.

For those of us who are parents, I deeply believe that next to leading our children to Christ, the greatest legacy we leave is that we have given our children a vision as to who they are in God.

3. Surrendering Our Critical and Pessimistic Tendencies is a Crucial Step to Overcoming Feelings of Inadequacy.

Christian psychological research has verified that if you battle with feelings of inadequacy, you often will tend to compensate for those low self-worth emotions by becoming critical toward others and becoming pessimistic in interpreting life events. Research further suggests that we can become cognitively confused and believe that if we tear another person down, that this action might lift us up in the eyes of others. This we can falsely believe will give us the approval we so desperately need because we have such strong feelings of inadequacy.

Accordingly, if a family member of another loved one conveys to you that you tend to have a critical or pessimistic spirit, this becomes a crucial matter to commit daily to God in prayer. It is of vital importance that we understand that a critical, pessimistic spirit can in all sorts of ways have a damaging impact on our spiritual and emotional well-being, as well as the impact it can have on the spiritual and emotional development of our families and other loved ones.

Many years ago, when I had moved away from home to study theology, optional chapel services were held three times a week at my university. Although chapel was scheduled at an early morning hour, and I had been up studying the night before, I decided to attend one particular chapel because I had heard from friends that the scheduled speaker was an outstanding preacher who had flown in from another city to speak.

I was disappointed with this pastor's message that morning. His sermon seemed disjointed and lacking in passion and inspiration. The speaker seemed distracted as he fumbled his way through is speech. On the way back to my dorm room after chapel, I said to a friend, "Boy, I was so disappointed in the pastor's message. I wish I had stayed in bed." My friend gently reprimanded me, saying, "Ron, I don't think you know all the facts. The pastor's son was killed in an automobile accident last night. Since the grieving father could not catch an earlier flight home, he still was willing to preach at chapel before flying to be with his bereaved wife."

"Ron, I don't think you know all the facts." It is no overstatement to suggest that this brief conversation was life changing for me. Countless times from that day forward, when I've been tempted to have a critical, pessimistic spirit toward another person, I've whispered to myself, "Ron you don't know all the facts. Loving God, protect me now from a critical spirit."

These three Biblical Principles are essential for each of us as we wrestle with feelings of inadequacy in our pilgrimage toward a life of joy:

1. **Acknowledging our inadequacies is a crucial step to becoming empowered by Jesus Christ and His love.**
2. **Seeing ourselves as God sees us is a crucial step to overcoming our feelings of inadequacy.**
3. **Surrendering our critical and pessimistic tendencies is a crucial step to overcoming feelings of inadequacy.**

Ed Farrell was visiting his uncle on his 80th birthday. Ed's uncle lived in Ireland, so Farrell flew from the United States to be with this wonderful man who had had such an impact on his life. Early in the morning on the first day of his visit, Ed Farrell's uncle climbed out of bed for a morning hike, as he had done every day for many years. As he walked around a scenic lake with his nephew, he whistled a happy tune. As he whistled, he would frequently break into a celebratory skip. At the midpoint of their hike on his uncle's 80th birthday, Ed asked, "Uncle, why has there always been so much joy in your life? As long as I've known you, there's been so much joy." Ed's uncle responded immediately in his endearing Irish accent, "'Oh, it's because The Father - He is so fond of me! My Heavenly Father is so fond of me!"

Do you know that? Do you know deeply in your heart *"Oh, The Father - He is so fond of me"*. For that reality will do so much to heal our feelings of inadequacy and enable us to choose joy.

Chapter 28

CHOOSING JOY IN THE MIDST OF LIFE'S GREATEST HEARTACHES

"James, a servant of God and of the Lord Jesus Christ, to the twelve tribes in the Dispersion: Greeting. Count it all joy, my brethren, when you meet various trials, for you know that the testing of your faith produces endurance. And let endurance have its full effect, that you may be mature and whole, lacking in nothing. If any of you lacks wisdom, let him ask God, who gives to all men generously and without reproaching, and it will be given to him. But let him ask in faith, with no doubting, for he who doubts is like a wave of the sea that is driven and tossed by the wind. For that person must not suppose that a double-minded man, unstable in all his ways, will receive anything from the Lord."

"Blessed is the man who endures trial, for when he has stood the test, he will receive the crown of life which God has promised to those who love him."
James 1:1-8, 12

It was pain that knocked upon my door
And said that she had come to stay
And though I would not welcome her
But begged her go away
She entered in
And like my own shade, she followed after me
And from her stabbing, stinging sword, no moment was I free.

In poetic words, we have just read a description of the reality of pain. As I read so many of your messages and emails sent to me each week, I am reminded of the words of Shakespeare: *"You are souls bruised with adversity."* And if we are Christian souls, we wrestle naturally with the question: *"When the bruises come, how are we to respond?"*

It's of great comfort to me to observe that this question is the catalyst for the very first topic James seeks to address in his very practical letter, 1 James 1:2. The author of the letter attempts to respond to a question that he knew was on the hearts of his Christian friends: "What am I supposed to do when the bruises come?" In the first century, the bruises were coming primarily in the form of physical persecution. In the first verse of James 1, James refers to the Christians who are dispersed or scattered. The reason these early Christians were scattered was because of oppression. These believers were often beaten for their faith, and as they were battered, they encountered bruises.

However, not all bruises are evident on the surface. Not all bruises are physical in nature. Some bruises come from deep down in our hearts, don't they? These are bruises of discouragement, disappointment, disillusionment and despair.

Some of you have been bruised by a friend who has betrayed you. Some of you may have been bruised by an unwanted divorce. Some of you may be bruised due to a diagnosis by your doctor that concerns you deeply. Perhaps some of you are bruised by the reality that you have a child who is far away from God or a loved one who battles addiction in its many forms. The list of bruises is a long and painful one.

Our first Biblical principle comes to us from James 1:2: *"Count it all joy, brethren, when you encounter various trials."*

1. Trials are inevitable.

Isn't it interesting that James doesn't say: "Count it all joy, brethren, *if* you encounter various trials?" No, James understands as a mature Christian that trials are inescapable.

Further, it may be helpful to note that the word we read in verse 2 that is translated as "various" is the same Greek term from which we get the word "polka dot". James is teaching us here that all of our lives will be polka dotted with different shapes and sizes of trials. For example, in my life, it may be a trial as minor as a head cold, or as major as living with chronic nerve pain for seven years due to scar tissue as a result of back surgery, or as devastating as the illness and death of my 41 year old brother. James makes clear to us that all types of trials will *polka dot* our lives. Trials are inevitable.

In James 1:3, we discover a second and more important Biblical Principle:

2. Trials are purposeful.

Trials are not only inevitable. Trials are purposeful. In this context, James in this passage is going to teach us both an immediate purpose and an ultimate purpose for our trials: *The immediate purpose of trials is to build endurance.*

The word we translate into English as endurance or steadfastness or perseverance literally means, "to abide under pressure." Perhaps you are going through a fire, you are going through a furnace, you are going through a trial. Endurance enables you to "abide under the pressure" of that trial and come out stronger than ever before in your life.

Some of you may have traveled to the Middle East. If so, you may have observed potters making vessels or jugs. The craftsman shapes the vessel, puts it through a fire, and if it does not crack, he stamps on the bottom of the pitcher or jar the Greek word, "*dokimos*", meaning "*approved.*" God yearns to help us go through even the most difficult fires of life with endurance so that He can stamp on our hearts "*dokimos*", "*approved*" — this man of God, this woman of God has endured the testing and come out stronger.

James goes on to not only give us an *immediate* purpose, but also an *ultimate* purpose for our trials. We discover this purpose in verse 4. Please notice the domino effect in this passage. James is writing that the finger of God comes into our lives, and He begins to push over the first domino of endurance as we battle a trial. Then this first domino of endurance bumps into a second domino of maturity, and that domino bumps into the third domino of character.

The ultimate purpose of trials is that our character will be made complete.

So now as Christians our perspective is transformed: when trials come into our lives, we no longer view these struggles as an enemy. Now we view these trials as a messenger, and this messenger comes to us with a note in his hand. We open the note and it reads: *"This trial has come for your endurance, and for your maturity so that your character might be complete."*

"Count it all joy", James writes in verse 2, and it is important to understand the meaning of the word "count" as it is translated into English from the New Testament Greek. The word, "count" literally means "to lead the way into something." It is the idea of the first float in a parade. James is teaching us that the leading thought for us to hold in our hearts when a trial enters our lives is joy!

This does not mean that we are happy when some tragedy comes into our lives. Rather, it is the reality that we understand deeply in our hearts that God is going to be teaching us lessons, and building endurance and maturity and character — so that we always come out stronger after we've been through the fire.

In this insightful passage, we next discover two reasons why we often do not respond correctly when trials invade our lives. These two reasons are given to us in James 1:5-8.

1. A Lack of Wisdom

James teaches us that if heartache touches our lives and we lack wisdom in knowing how to respond to it, we are to ask God in prayer for His guidance. What is wisdom? For the Christian, simply stated, *wisdom is the ability to view all of life from God's perspective.*

A trial, big or small, enters our lives. Our prayer immediately becomes, "Loving God, help me to understand this trial not from *my* vantage point, but from *Your* vantage point." That's wisdom!

2. A Lack of Faith

James teaches us that the second reason why we are very often lacking in a correct response to trials that come into our lives is because of a lack of faith. In verse 6-8 James challenges us to become men and women of faith when trials enter our lives so that now we understand that when struggles disrupt our lives:

- A lack of wisdom causes us to become confused.
- A lack of faith causes us to become overwhelmed.

Put another way, wisdom is gaining God's insight for the trial. Faith is gaining God's strength to endure the trial. So that from this day forward, when a trial enters our lives, we first pray for wisdom because we yearn for God's perspective on the trial. Secondly, we pray for faith because we know we need the strength to endure the trial so that it does not overwhelm us.

Three final principles of application for our lives this week:

1. When trials come, look up and be comforted by God's love.

The Old Testament figure Job models the principles we uncover in James. Job was able to "count it all joy" because in the midst of his trials, he was able to say: *"The Lord giveth, the Lord taketh away. Blessed be the name of the Lord. Shall we receive good at the hand of God and shall we also not receive trial?"* Job was able to "count it all joy" because he looked up to the Love of God.

2. When trials come, look ahead and be reminded of God's promises.

Job, in the midst of the devastating trial of the loss of his children remembered the promises about 'what the future would be like', and so he said, "*I know that my Redeemer liveth and at the last day He shall stand up on the earth. After my skin has been destroyed, then I shall with my face see God.*" Job could "count it all joy" because he could look ahead to the future promises — just as the Apostle Paul did when he wrote in Romans 8:18: "*I reckon that the sufferings of this present moment cannot be compared with the glory that shall be revealed to us.*" When trials enter our lives, we can look forward and be reminded of God's promises.

3. When trials come, look within and be shaped by God's Wisdom.

It is of crucial importance that each of us make the decision now that when trials come into our lives that we will be guided by God's wisdom as found in Scripture.

Doug Coe was, for many years, the Director of a Nationwide Christian Movement known as the Fellowship. When Doug Coe's son, Jonathan, was 28 years old, he was diagnosed with a type of severe cancer that would take his life. I saw a copy of the memorial service program that was printed for Jonathan Coe. On one side of the program, there was an order of worship for the service. On the other side of the program, there were these words printed on the page: "These were the first words that Jonathan Coe said after he heard the diagnosis from his doctor: 'For me, the challenge isn't living or dying, because either way, I win. For me, the challenge is obedience to Christ in whatever time I have left.'"

A 28-year-old with a rare maturity in Christ reflecting the teachings of James Chapter 1: "*Either way I win.*"

It was pain that knocked upon my door
And said that she had come to stay
And though I would not welcome her
But begged her go away
She entered in
And like my own shade she followed after me
And from her stabbing, stinging sword
No moment was I free

But do we realize the poet doesn't stop there? There is a second verse, a final verse:

And then one day another knocked
Most gently at my door
I said, "No! Pain is here! There is no room for more!"
And then I heard His Tender Voice
"It is I. Be not afraid."
And from the day Christ entered in
Oh, the difference He has made.

And the difference is joy.

"Count it all joy when you encounter various trials."
James 1:1

Chapter 29

CHOOSING JOY IN THE MIDST OF LIFE'S STORMS

Richard and LeeAnn Acosta built their lives on the rock of Jesus Christ. A storm moved into the lives of their family that would test how solid their foundation was going to be. In a letter to their friends, Richard and LeeAnn vulnerably write about their heart-breaking tempest:

> *Our son Stevie was a special gift from God. He was given a good, strong body, an inquisitive mind, and a warm and tender heart for both people and animals. His last task from his hospital bed was finding a good family for each of his six curly, black-haired puppies.*
>
> *We were so proud of our gallant little fellow who fought so bravely: "Please read to me, Mommie, from my Bible." "Daddy, when it hurts so much that I get afraid, I ask God for courage, and He always helps me through."*
>
> *Stevie's time was short. His daddy took him on Thursday, September 12 to the hospital. He had one completely collapsed lung. For ten days, the pulmonary specialist tried to restore his lungs, but his efforts were hindered by a tumor which gave the doctor reason for suspicion. An exploratory operation of the abdomen confirmed that our Stevie suffered from a malignant cancer which had invaded his whole system.*
>
> *On Saturday morning, September 28, both of us in a circle of love and prayer, accompanied our little boy to the entrance of this other existence where pain and sadness have lost their power. Early on Sunday morning, Richard discovered in our yard a beautiful orchid blossom. We had brought these plants from Hawaii, but the California climate was not suitable for them. So many times Richard had admonished Stevie to water them more often, but they seemed so sad and dry to*

us that we had given up hope on them. But then there appeared this beautiful blossom on the day of Stevie's departure, and a second one on the day of his burial. It was like Stevie's laughter saying to us in his loving way, 'Mom and Dad, life has more power than death.'

The Memorial service was led by our pastor. He directed our eyes to the life everlasting and when he asked, 'Will we see our loved one again?', Markus, Stevie's little brother who was very lonely for Stevie, nodded his head vigorously in affirmation. Hymns of faith resounded in the chapel, and something wonderful, like the joy and victory of Easter morning, entered our hearts."

The Acosta Family, mourning with empty arms, found strength in the midst of this horrendous tragedy, because they built their faith on The Rock.

In this chapter, I want to share about the joy that can be found when we build our lives on the rock of Jesus Christ. Further, I will use the powerful story that Jesus gave us at the conclusion of *The Sermon on the Mount* as the foundation for my reflections.

In Matthew 7:24-29, we read this familiar story:

"Therefore everyone who hears these words of mine, and puts them into practice is like a wise man who built his house on the rock. The rain came down, the streams rose, and the winds blew and beat against that house; yet, it did not fall because it had its foundation on the rock. But, everyone who hears these words of mine, and does not put them into practice is like a foolish man who built his house on sand. The rain came down, the streams rose, and the winds blew and beat against that house, and it fell with a great

crash. When Jesus had finished saying these things, the crowds were amazed at his teaching, because he taught as one who had authority, and not as their teachers of the law."

I have been an author long enough to know that you may not remember any other idea that I will share in this chapter, but, for years to come, you will recall the courageous true story of Stevie Acosta and his family. From the time I was a little boy, I was intrigued by the power of a story. Some stories are rooted in history. Some stories come to us from novels, films or plays. On a deeper level, many stories are analogies or metaphors or similes.

Frequently, stories that we share come from our own lives, don't they? They come from our past. They come from our childhood. My mother was a widow for thirty-seven years before her death, and for many of those years, she lived with me. Often, in the evenings, Mom and I would share stories about our family and friends as we flipped through old photo albums. Wonderful stories!

Jesus Christ was the greatest storyteller in human history. In Matthew 13, we read that Jesus actually preferred telling stories as a teaching method. Jesus was never one who spoke to people in complex, theoretical, elaborate or vague words. Rather, he spoke about a loving Father who forgave his wayward son. He spoke about a farmer sowing seeds on a hillside. He spoke about a good man who helped someone who had been beaten by robbers. He told stories.

In fact, by the time we arrive at Matthew 13:3, we read that Jesus, in his teaching, told only stories. Except the word that is used in the Greek text, here is not the word "story." It is the word "parable." The word parable comes from the Greek term "parabole". *Para*, meaning "alongside". Bolé meaning "to cast." To cast alongside.

The teller of a parable is one who literally casts something alongside something else. He casts something that is unfamiliar alongside something that is very familiar, and in doing so, the unfamiliar takes on a new and deeper meaning than we have ever experienced before. For example, when Jesus says in Matthew 13:24, *"The Kingdom of God is like the farmer who plants crops in his field,"* our Lord casts alongside something unfamiliar to many (the Kingdom of God) with something very familiar to many (planting crops in a field.) This is how Jesus taught, and by the time we turn to Matthew 13:34 we read, *"All that Jesus said to the crowds was in parables. He said nothing to them without a parable"* — without a story.

Jesus comes to the conclusion of the greatest sermon ever preached in human history. Please notice Jesus does not end his message with ambiguous sentimentality. He ends his teaching with a story, a parable, a storm warning. He ends with a cautionary tale about whether we are really building our lives on a firm foundation.

First, it is crucial to observe in this story that Jesus is *not* teaching that there will never be storms in the life of the Christian. The storms come to both the wise man and the foolish man. *Storms are inevitable!*

Jesus is not teaching in this story how to avoid life's storms. Rather, he is teaching us how to build a faith that is going to get us *through* the storms. He is not teaching us first of all how to pray for safety. He is teaching us how to pray for *maturity*. He is not teaching to pray for a painless life. He is teaching us to pray for a *productive* life.

Notice the similarities and the contrasts between the two men in the story. Both men are building a house. They are evidently in the same general location, perhaps in close proximity to one another. The men have to face the same storm.

In a spiritual sense, we might suggest they are similar to two Christians who go to the same church and Bible study, and proclaim the same Lord. It is, in fact, very hard to distinguish between these two Christians — *until the storm comes!* Then we are able to distinguish between the man who is building on the rock, and the one who is building on the sand.

Now notice the contrasts between these two men. While both men are building houses, and both men are facing a storm — beyond these realities, the story is a study in contrasts. Builder #1 has not only heard Christ's message, he has acted on it. *That is the difference!*

As we live out our lives, most of us can do pretty well in our daily pilgrimage until a storm enters our lives. What *are* the storms?

- It is a painful waiting time as we anxiously hold on for the results of tests related to a serious health concern.
- It is the pain of a divorce we never dreamed we would have to face.
- It may be a family member who is far away from God.
- It is the pain of addiction in our own lives or the life of a loved one.
- It may be the reality that we are growing older, and as we age, we battle a loss of mental acuity or periodic depression.

Some of us have had the experience of visiting someone who is critically ill in the hospital, and then saying to a friend after our visit, "When I went to the hospital, I wanted to minister to that person, but as I left the hospital I realized that that person had ministered to me." Very often, this reality is because the person who is hospitalized has built his life on The Rock, not on the sand.

C.S. Lewis stated it well when, after his beloved wife's death from cancer, he wrote in his diary: *"If my house has collapsed with one blow, it is because it was a house made out of cards."* In other words, if my life, my faith, my family collapses with one blow, from one storm in life, perhaps it is because my faith has not been built on The Rock.

Two eternal principles of application emerge from this powerful story told by Jesus centuries ago:

1. **If we are only *hearing* the truth, we are not preparing for life's storms.**

One man in this story was a wise man because he *acted* on what he heard. And we choose to act because we understand that Christ did not die so that we wouldn't suffer. He died so that our suffering might be like his suffering. What was Christ's suffering like? It was purposeful! It was redemptive! It was sacrificial! It was meaningful!

So now when any storm comes into our lives, we yearn to become the type of mature Christians who go before our loving God and pray, *"Heavenly Father, take this storm that has come into my life and as I work in partnership with you, as I act in collaboration with you, transform this storm into something that will bring purpose, meaning and hope to others."* If we are only *hearing* the truth — without acting on it — we are not preparing for life's storms.

2. **If our foundation is strong, no storm will cause our life to collapse.**

A storm may very well jolt us and we may feel the blows. But the good news is that our house is going to stand!

Elisabeth Elliot faced a severe storm in her life years ago. After her husband and four other missionaries were murdered by Auca Indians in Ecuador, Elisabeth made a decision to bring good out of a seemingly senseless tragedy. Courageously she chose to offer her trial of grief and discouragement to God so that He could transform it into ministry to others. After many weeks in prayer, she sensed that God was leading her to go to the Aucas who had killed her husband, Jim Elliot and carry on his work among them.

Months later, Elisabeth stood in the Auca village which had been her husband's objective, sharing the gospel with the same men who had murdered the five missionaries. Touched by her forgiveness and love, these men gave their hearts to Christ, and were later baptized in the river where the slaughter had taken place. Next, the Aucas themselves baptized the children of Jim Elliot and the other slain missionaries. That day, the waters that had once flowed with the blood of martyrs became a river of healing and forgiveness.

But the story doesn't end there. The Auca Christians were so transformed by the forgiveness and love that had been modeled toward them, that they decided to go to an enemy tribe downstream, and tell them of the love of Christ. They set off into danger — armed only with the gospel of peace.

The Aucas arrived at the encampment of the other tribe and were met by fierce warriors armed with arrows and spears. The Auca Christians offered no resistance, only love and forgiveness. One of them, named Tona, stood in his boat saying over and over to his enemies, "I forgive you! I forgive you! I am dying for your benefit!" Those were his last words before he was slain.

But even this is not the end of the story. This fierce downriver tribe, like the Aucas before them, ultimately yielded to the forgiving love of Christ. On and on, the gospel spread through this remote region of Ecuador, just as the gospel has spread throughout Christian history.

God uses people like you and me, even in our most painful and discouraging storms, to influence others and work out His plan. We are to joyfully demonstrate to a watching world what Christian men and women are really like away from the safety of the harbor and placed right in the midst of a storm.

Chapter 30

CHOOSING JOY AS WE BECOME WOUNDED HEALERS

Throughout the 1920's, '30s, and '40s, Kathleen Thompson Norris dominated the best-seller lists with such romantic novels as *Belle-Mere, Shining Windows*, and *Storm House*. Few of her millions of readers, however, knew of the tragedy that marked her earlier life. At the age of nineteen, Kathleen suffered the double tragedy of losing both her mother and father within a month of each other. Although she found happiness again the next year when she married novelist Charles Norris, and subsequently gave birth to two lovely daughters and a little boy, tragedy was soon to strike once more.

Within one three-week period, both of Kathleen's little girls died of influenza and pneumonia. Devastated by her loss, Kathleen convinced Charles they should move from San Francisco to New York City, and start a new life. There, she threw herself into her writing, completing three new novels during her first year in New York. While her writing met with critical acclaim and commercial success, she could not escape the nagging sense of unhappiness and emptiness left by the loss of her "little darlings."

During this time, a friend told Kathleen of an "unsanctioned" baby — the child of an unwed mother — being cared for at Bellevue Hospital. Kathleen went to the hospital and fell in love with the baby at first sight. That same day, she had adoption papers drawn. After two weeks of hospital care, the baby would be hers to take home.

Kathleen visited the infant every day. When two weeks had nearly passed, she was told the baby had developed an infection and would need to stay a couple days longer. When she arrived before noon the next day, however, she was met by the head nurse. "I don't know quite how to tell you this, Mrs. Norris, but —"

Kathleen could see the terrible news in the nurse's eyes. The baby had died.

The nurse put her arm around Kathleen's shoulders and continued to talk, easing her into a chair. Kathleen barely heard the nurse's next words. "People are born and people die in this hospital every day," the nurse said, "but I never get used to the job of breaking bad news. Why, at this very moment, there's a little boy in the next room whose mother died not half an hour ago. He doesn't know it yet, poor thing, and now somebody has to tell him that he's all alone in the world. I don't suppose —" The nurse hesitated.

"What?" Kathleen looked up suddenly. "Do you want me to tell the boy his mother died?"

"It was a foolish thought," said the nurse. "I had no right to ask—"

"Actually, I think it's a very good idea," Kathleen said. "I would like to tell him."

After drying her eyes and composing herself, she went with the nurse to the doorway of a nearby waiting room. Then, with a smile and a casual air, she strode into the next room and met a worried-looking eight-year-old boy. "Well, hello there! What's your name?" she asked brightly.

"Billy."

"Well, Billy, I'm Mrs. Norris. I'm very hungry, but I simply hate to eat alone. Aren't you hungry, too? There's a nice place to eat just on the next block. Would you like to have lunch with me, Billy?"

"I don't know," the boy said dubiously. "My mother might wake up, and she's gonna want to see me. The nurse promised to call me if she—"

"Well, I'll tell the nurse where we'll be. Then, if your mother wakes up" — she paused to steady her voice — "if she wakes up, the nurse will call us at the restaurant."

"Well — Okay."

Kathleen and Billy got along fine through lunch. She even persuaded the boy to go with her to the hotel where she lived. There, she showed him some books that belonged to her own little boy. Outside, the sky was just beginning to darken. Billy said, "I think I should be going now. My mother may be waking up."

Kathleen knew the time had come. "Billy," she said slowly, "there's something I have to tell you." A few hours earlier, he would have learned of his mother's death from a stranger. Now he heard it from a friend. And in the coming years, he grew up in the home of this friend.

Billy grew up to become Bill Norris, a well-known newspaper reporter on the West Coast, and Kathleen loved him as her own son. Though she never forgot the particular string of each of her tragic losses — her parents, her little girls, and the baby she loved but never took home — Kathleen Norris experienced the healing joy of reaching out to another hurting soul in the midst of her own sorrow. She discovered how to transform her hurt by reaching beyond herself and her own hurts, by touching the hurts of a grieving little boy.

That's the lesson you and I can learn as we endeavor to move beyond the trials and heartaches of life. When we've suffered hurt, there is tremendous therapeutic value in finding a cause greater than ourselves to which we can commit. If we have no greater cause than seeking our own happiness, we will ultimately become absorbed and obsessed with self. When a self-absorbed person suffers mistreatment, self-pity inevitably follows. We will never be free of the tyranny of the past until we are free of the tyranny of self.

One saying of Christ is recorded in all four Gospels, Matthew, Mark, Luke, and John: *"Whoever finds his life will lose it, and whoever loses his life for my sake will find it."* I've seen the truth of that statement proved over and over again: those who try to "find" themselves, who try to get "into" themselves, almost always end up losing themselves by sinking into a morass of confusion, alienation, and self-pity. But those who get out of themselves, who "lose" themselves in service to God and to others, almost invariably find themselves. They discover new strengths and abilities, new levels of understanding, new facets of character deep within themselves. Most of all, they find they simply have no time for self-pity.

With that as our focus, we can see that the trials we have suffered are not just random, meaningless wounds. Rather, these wounds become a resource we can use to help heal the hurts of those around us. We actually find healing in our own souls as we make our own experiences — both our pain and our joy — available to others to help them gain insight and healing for their hurts.

Moreover, the heartaches you and I have suffered give us the authority and authenticity to help others who are hurting. Our painful experiences enable us to speak as people who have lived not in an ivory tower, but in the trenches of life. As Henri Nouwen observed in his book, *The Wounded Healer:*

> *"Who can save a child from a burning house without taking the risk of being hurt by the flames? Who can listen to a story of loneliness and despair without taking the risk of experiencing similar pains in his own heart and even losing his precious peace of mind? In short: Who can take away suffering without entering it? The great illusion is to think that a man can be led out of the desert by someone who has never been there."*

Because you have been to the desert of grief, you have received a great gift. You now have the gift of empathy. You know what it is like to be deeply wounded. That gives you the right and the authority to talk to others who have been deeply hurt by life. You have a depth of understanding and insight that few others have. By using your experience of suffering instead of simply trying to escape it, you can find the truest form of emotional wholeness and freedom. You can witness the miraculous transformation of hurt into healing. And when you experience this Christ-like perspective, you discover the joyful pilgrimage of becoming a wounded healer.

Chapter 31

CHOOSING JOY AS WE MAKE OUR LIVES ACTS OF LOVE

Years ago, two renowned psychologists conducted an intriguing research project. A group of theology students at Princeton Theological Seminary were given an assignment. These budding Bible students were to generate a brief sermon based on the Parable of The Good Samaritan as recorded in Luke 10. These students, all preparing to become pastors, were given time slots and the specific classroom where they would preach. The psychologists then hired an actor to portray a fatigued and sick man who was given the assignment of laying in the hallway where each student would have to pass by on the way to their assigned class. Nine out of every ten students, perceived this seemingly critically ill man, but went out of their way to pass by him so that they could arrive for their assigned preaching presentation on time! In other words, nine out of ten professing Christians, on their way to preach a sermon on The Parable of the Good Samaritan, failed to be a good Samaritan to an apparently hurting and broken person.

Throughout the Book of Acts, we discover no such dichotomy between words and actions. Rather, we recognize a powerful congruence between the message that is shared verbally and the lives being lived out by these 1st Century Christians. We discover a specific example of this reality in Acts 3 where we encounter a man who is crippled physically and broken spiritually. This man has been carried to the temple gate, where he would sit each day to beg for money. This disabled man did not know the joy there is in standing erect. But more than being physically crippled, he was spiritually crippled as well, lacking in purpose.

George Bernard Shaw wrote, *"Every man is ill at ease until he finds his purpose."* Friedrich Nietzsche stated, *"He who has a 'why' to live can bear any 'how'"*. That is to say that if we know our purpose, our calling, that will empower us dramatically as we face life's greatest trials. Dietrich Bonhoeffer, suffering in a Nazi prison camp, less than a year away from his execution, penned these words: *"In view of our Supreme Purpose, this present difficulty we face seems trivial."* Trivial! Because Bonhoeffer knew his purpose!

The crippled man in Acts 2 had no such purpose. Perhaps some of you today may also feel unclear about your life's mission. Maybe you even feel shelved, backed into a corner, battling a tragic circumstance, discouraged in some area of your life, spiritually crippled. I believe that the same Christ who brought healing to a crippled man 2,000 years ago can offer his *Touch of Restoration* to all of us — and enable us to live our lives as Acts of Love.

In Acts 3:3, we encounter a crippled man holding out his hand as Peter and John walk past him. Peter says to the man, "I do not have silver or gold, but what I have, I give to you. In the name of Christ, walk!" Immediately, the paralytic is healed. Peter and John told the disabled beggar they would not give him what he wanted — money. Rather, they would give him what he needed — healing. The same reality is so often true in our own prayers. We don't always get what we want. However, we are given what we need — for our growth, for our healing, for our character development, so that we might become more like Christ.

I deeply believe that God yearns for each of us to become, like Peter and John, joyful agents of healing for those who are spiritually, emotionally, relationally or physically crippled in our homes, with our loved ones, in our churches and communities. When we intentionally choose to seek to bring God's healing touch to others, we make our lives nothing less than Acts of Love. I want to suggest four practical principles that will better enable each of us to become agents of healing grace to broken people all around us:

1. **Be willing to become deeply involved in the lives of broken and hurting people.**
As you may know, years ago Dr. Elizabeth Kubler-Ross wrote an insightful book entitled *On Death and Dying*, which sketches in the

five stages of what a grieving person often faces in the midst of their own impending death or the imminent death of a loved one. For many years, Dr. Kubler-Ross was the head of staff for a group of psychiatrists on the East Coast who were seeking to minister to dying patients. Dr. Kubler-Ross became discouraged because she sensed most of the professional psychiatrists were unable to truly break through and give hope to the patients with terminal illnesses.

Dr. Kubler-Ross closely observed that while she was cleaning their rooms, the cleaning lady was giving hope to the patients. Dr. Kubler-Ross closely observed the cleaning lady over a period of time in the days that followed as this woman gave hope to the patients in the process of cleaning their rooms. Finally, Dr. Kubler-Ross approached the cleaning lady and asked, "What's your secret? How are you able to impact our patients?" The cleaning lady responded softly, "Oh, there is no secret. I just go into the hospital rooms and I see these people who are so afraid. I'm not afraid of death anymore. My little boy died in my arms of pneumonia when he was only three years old. So when I feel led by God, I go up to these people, and I listen to them, and I hug them and I love them."

Dr. Elizabeth Kubler-Ross immediately appointed the cleaning lady as her assistant head of staff with oversight over all of the psychiatrists in the hospital, much to their chagrin and dismay. Here was a Christian woman who had yielded her life to the power of our loving God so that she could become a healing agent as she chose to become deeply involved in the lives of hurting people. In so doing, this uneducated cleaning lady had transformed her life into an Act of Love.

Over several decades of ministering with many people, I have observed that we are so often ineffective in truly impacting a loved one because we are unwilling to become authentically, deeply involved in the broken person's life. If we would truly enable our lives to become Acts of Love, we must make the risky decision to walk closely alongside those who are broken and hurting.

2. Be willing, at the appropriate time, to courageously, tenderly teach the Great Christian Truths to the broken person.

It was Carl Rogers who is remembered as *"The Father of Non-Directive Counseling"*. In his own counseling, Dr. Rogers was often very directive and involved with troubled people. However, many of his disciples misrepresented his lectures to such an extreme that in many counseling centers and churches around the country, therapists and pastors very rarely give any direction to hurting people. Rather, they simply listen and affirm, and become totally non-directive in all their interactions with the crippled person.

In contrast to this view, the Christian who is seeking to make his life an Act of Love to hurting people will understand that the New Testament Greek word for counseling (*noutheteo*) literally means "to teach." Accordingly, "non-directive counseling" is for the Christian a contradiction in terms. If we are seeking to make our lives an Act of Love, we recognize that we simply cannot be totally non-directive when a struggling loved one asks for our guidance and support.

As Christians, we know that we are to yearn to grow in wisdom, and that we understand that wisdom is *"viewing all of life from God's perspective."* We grow in wisdom as we learn Scriptural principles and apply them to the common life problems we and our loved ones face.

As I have ministered with men both within the church and on professional sports teams, I've observed compulsive, addictive behavior that either currently is or will become very destructive to my friend's lives. One question I've often asked is: *"Have you deeply reflected on the pain you will bring to yourself and to your loved ones if you continue to walk down this path?"* To say nothing would be to fail to live life as an Act of Love.

3. **Be ready to place an emphasis on present difficulties and future responsibilities as you interact with loved ones who are struggling in some arena of their lives.**

As you may know, there has been a growing tendency in our culture to blame our present behavior exclusively on our past conditioning and childhood experiences. A Christian seeking to make his or her life an Act of Love will generally seek to challenge the broken loved one to examine specific present difficulties and future responsibilities.

Dr. Hobart Mowrer, in a scathing attack on much of contemporary culture and related counseling methods writes, *"The success of the blame game, with all its' emphasis on the past, and the blaming of people in our past so common in conventional counseling, seemed complete. Only one thing went wrong. The hurting person did not get any better."*

For many of us, our parents did the best they could. Like us, they were flawed, and made poor decisions at times. But even if you grew up in a family system where your parents blatantly violated their responsibility, then God would still have us come to a place where in our hearts we absolutely believe His Good can come from this pain as we become Wounded Healers forging out our lives as Acts of Love.

The Apostle Paul writes in Philippians 3:13-14, *"This one thing I do, forgetting those things that are in the past and reaching forward to what lies ahead, I press on toward the mark for the prize of the high calling of God in Christ Jesus."* Throughout the New Testament there is this emphasis that the past is over, and we are now to take full and complete responsibility for our present choices and the consequences of those choices.

The Christian who truly yearns to make his or her life an Act of Love will place an emphasis on present difficulties and future responsibilities — and encourage his loved ones to model this pattern as well.

4. Be ready to encourage your hurting loved ones to reject isolation and to bond with positive Christian friends.

Dr. Philip Zimbardo, a renowned psychologist and professor at Stanford University writes,

> *"I know of no more potent killer than isolation. There is no more destructive influence on our physical and mental health than the isolation of you from me. It has been shown to be a central agent in the diagnosis of depression, paranoia, schizophrenia, suicide and a wide variety of other diseases."*

For many of us, especially men, there is a tendency to isolate from our family and friends when we are going through a valley of struggle, disillusionment or pain. Generally, this is the worst possible choice we can make for our own spiritual, emotional, and physical heath.

Dr. Kelly McGonigal in her audiobook *The Science of Compassion*, provides overwhelming research that links isolation with increased risk of illness and a shorter life span. If we genuinely yearn to make our lives Acts of Love, we will intentionally reach out to isolated loved ones, and with arms of compassion, welcome them into our families.

One friend who reached out to me in a season of my life when I was prone to isolate was Bill Lennard. Bill invited me to join him for a Christian conference in Houston, Texas years ago. During one of the sessions at the conference, author Lyman Coleman asked us to turn to a friend and give as a symbolic gift some token of love and affection. All around me, I overheard the conference participants sharing with one another statements like, "Here's my business card.

If you are even in Des Moines, please give me a call." Or "Here's a bracelet my granddaughter made for me. I want you to have it as a remembrance of our days together here in Texas."

My friend, Bill Lennard, pulled out his wallet and fumbled his way through various cards and dollar bills. Finally, he pulled out one particular card. It was a Red Cross Donor Card with his blood type printed on it. Bill then said softly to me, "Ron, this card represents my blood, and my blood represents my life. I want you to know I love you, and I would be willing to lay my life down for you." And he meant it. He lived his life that way. And when he died, many rose up and called him Blessed.

Bill Lennard lived his life as an Act of Love. Will we?

Chapter 32

CHOOSING JOY AS WE HEAL BROKEN RELATIONSHIPS

One of my dear friends shared with me a moving experience that happened in his life a few years after we had both graduated from the same seminary. Steve was a creative pastor serving in his first congregation. From the outset of his ministry at the church, he sought to bring about a number of innovative changes in:

- the style of worship
- the structure of youth ministry
- the children's Sunday School program
- the selection of hymns and praise choruses sung on Sunday morning

Almost immediately Steve began to experience significant conflict within his congregation, particularly with an elderly gentleman who served on the church's leadership board. Steve and the aging board member differed on nearly every major issue that was brought before the church Elder Board. Yet, the two of them quickly became close friends. They golfed together. They met weekly for dinner at a local restaurant. They enjoyed taking in movies regularly at the local theatre.

This close relationship puzzled some members of the local congregation. Finally, after several months, one church member asked the elderly gentleman, "Could you help me understand your friendship with our new pastor? The two of you seem to disagree on nearly every issue and yet you seem to be the best of friends." The board member replied softly, "Oh, it's not really too difficult to understand. When our new pastor first came to serve at our church my beloved wife was dying of cancer. When she became very ill and was near death, our young pastor sat with me and my wife for 24 hours, holding my wife's hand with one of his hands and holding my hand with his other hand, as she passed from this life into eternity. Out of that deeply moving and compassionate experience, we began to build a relationship of love with one another centered in Jesus Christ that covers all our differences."

I passionately believe that the attitude and perspective of that elderly gentleman reflects exactly the message of Jesus Christ in the Gospels. Our Lord's final request in prayer on the night before the cross was simply that we might all be one — united through our shared love for Christ (see John 17:20-23.) Further, Jesus teaches in this passage that our love for one another will be our most powerful witness before a watching world.

Because I knew from John 17 and other Gospel passages that unity, reconciliation and love for one another were such passionate concerns from the very heart of God, I developed years ago ten Biblically based principles that I would covenant to review each time I knew I was about to embark upon a loving confrontation.

I share these ten guidelines with you, certain that if you build these truths into the fabric of your character, they will serve you well whenever you care enough to confront someone you love.

1. Go to the person in an attitude of prayer and humility.

A situation arises in your life where you know, as a matter of obedience and integrity, you must face someone in your family, your neighborhood, your work or your church family. Immediately you decide to go to the person in an attitude of **prayer** and **humility**.

- Prayer – seeking wisdom from our loving God
- Humility – deeply aware of your brokenness and shortcomings

The single most helpful prayer throughout my life as I have prepared for loving confrontation has always been the prayer of St. Francis. Seeking to offer each word from my heart, I pray the opening section of the prayer:

> *"Lord, make me an instrument of your peace. Where there is hatred, let me sow love. Where there is injury, pardon. Where there is doubt, faith. Where there is despair, hope. Where there is darkness, light."*

2. Be Gentle

Galatians 6:1 is clear at this point: *"Whenever you seek to loving-ly confront someone, it must be done in a spirit of gentleness."* (Paraphrase). The explicit teaching of Scripture is that if we can't go to a family member or friend in gentleness, then we ought not go at all. As I am preparing for a loving confrontation, I often quote to myself over and over proverbs 15:1: *"A soft answer turns away wrath."*

3. Be certain that you fully understand the situation.

Research indicates that in general terms, men are less effective in this area than women. So, for example, when a father addresses a conflict that has taken place with two of his children, he needs to be asking himself the question as he knocks on the door of his child's room, *"Do I know the whole story?"* Maybe the father has heard part of the story from the child's sister, but before any kind of discipline or confrontation takes place, the father wants to be certain that he knows the whole story from his child.

This third principle is so important that Stephen Covey in his classic book *The 7 Habits of Highly Effective People* lists this as the fifth habit: ***"First seek to understand, then to be understood."*** He states that of the seven habits, this is the most difficult to apply where there is a broken relationship or need for loving confrontation.

4. Verbally affirm your love for the other person regularly, and throughout the conversation.

As Christians, we are to affirm verbally and non-verbally that we are absolutely committed to the other person, no matter how distaste-ful or offensive their behavior has been. We do this because we know that this person is created in the image of God. We do this because we are seeking to see this person through the eyes of Jesus. We do this because we know the goal of the conversation is to restore the person we love, and we understand that in the Greek text the word "restore" literally means "to mend the brokenness.'

One question that we can always ask ourselves as the conversation is concluded is: *"Did the other person feel valued during our interaction?"* One crucial way that we validate a family member or friend where there is a conflict or an inappropriate behavior that needs to be confronted is to constantly reassure that person of our love for them.

5. As you seek to lovingly confront a friend or family member, always remind yourself that the other person may become defensive.

Throughout my life, it has often been my responsibility to confront loved ones who are involved in broken lifestyles or addictive, compulsive behaviors that are bringing great pain to themselves and their families. At times, these friends or a family member will become belligerent and defensive. In our own human nature, when the person becomes enraged and angry, we often can respond with the same harsh tone. But if we are praying within our hearts throughout the confrontation for the empowering of God's love and compassion, then we can remain calm and patient even in the midst of the anger and indignation that we may experience in our loved one who is being confronted.

6. Be very specific.

For example, in a family setting, far better to say softly, "You know, Son, I feel that you were deceptive with me when you didn't tell me the whole story of all the places you were going last night" — than to say loudly, "You are nothing but a liar! You will never be anything but a liar!" We at times need to critique the behavior of a loved one, but we never need to shame the person.

7. Ask God to help you look past the irritation to the need.

A wise Christian is always seeking to look deeper than just the inappropriate or irritating behavior of a loved one because he yearns to discover the root need of the person. Is my loved one insecure? Is he or she crying out for help, and doesn't have the maturity to know how to express their hurt in any other way than through inappropriate behavior? Few principles have been more helpful to me as a pastor, parent, friend, than this guideline: *"Look past the irritation to the need."*

8. Recognize that it often takes much longer to heal a relationship than to hurt it.

As we have all experienced, a loving relationship that has taken years to build can be deeply harmed in an instant. Because we understand this reality, we recognize that sometimes after a loving confrontation has taken place, the wisest action to take is to just put our arm around our loved one, reaffirm our love for that person, and then for a time withdraw. We do this because we want to give our loved one some time to work through their feelings — there may be tears — there may be some bitterness toward us for caring enough to confront. Because we understand the relational dynamic that it often takes longer to heal a relationship than to hurt it, we give our loved ones some space for a period of time – due to our love for them.

9. Remind yourself throughout your loving confrontation that God yearns for us to be deeply concerned about our own character development and the character development of our loved ones.

A.B. Bruce, an insightful and courageous 19th century pastor, once wrote, *"None are more formidable instruments of temptation than well-meaning friends who care more about your comfort than your character."* Put another way, there are few choices that a Christian can make that are more tragic than to care more about our loved one's comfort than the development of his or her character. We are in this pilgrimage with our loved ones through all eternity, and it is God's intention for each of us that we help one another become all that we are meant to be in Christ.

10. The purpose of loving confrontation is to heal, not to cripple. It is to restore, not to shame.

A beloved friend, pastor and mentor to me for many years modeled this tenth principle in his congregation many years ago. My pastor friend realized he needed to lovingly confront a member of his congregation who lacked integrity over a long period of time in one area of his life. My pastor friend lovingly stood by this man for a period of five years, even as he gently, consistently confronted his moral failure. Finally, this man authentically acknowledged his painful pattern of deception and sent a letter to my pastor friend with a request that the letter be printed in the church newsletter. The letter read as follows:

> *"My fellow Christians, several years ago our pastor held me accountable in love for a lack of integrity in an area of my life. The concerns raised about my lifestyle were completely true. I cannot reverse history and undo all the events that led to my moral failure. I have harmed many people and brought heartache to my family and to myself.*
>
> *After I became a Christian many years ago, I failed to deal thoroughly with certain character flaws in my life. In time, I became self-deceived, proud and arrogant. I am in need of your prayers and your forgiveness for I have wronged each of you. I am await-*

ing further grace and mercy from God in this matter and now know that our pastor's confrontation was done out of love for me and for all of you." (Letter edited to maintain confidentiality)

Having received this letter and printed it in the church newsletter, my pastor friend called for a special Sunday evening service. After several hymns and praise choruses were sung, my friend called this man to come down to the platform. Using the symbols from the parable of the prodigal Son, my pastor friend said to this man, "I have a new robe for you", and he wrapped a robe around the shoulders of the man. Then he said, "I have a new ring for you", and he slipped a beautiful ring on the man's finger. Finally, my friend said, "I have some new shoes for you", and the pastor knelt down and put the shoes on his repentant friend's feet.

After the worship service, a large celebration dinner was held in the fellowship hall of the church. This man had been fully restored through loving confrontation where the clear goal was to heal, not cripple. It was to restore, not to shame.

May all of us live our lives with such love whenever situations arise where we must care enough to confront. When we live daily and fully a life of loving concern for others who stumble, we will experience restoration, healing and joy.

Chapter 33

CHOOSING JOY BY DISCOVERING A LIFE OF SERENITY

My beloved father, a Presbyterian pastor, loved to tell the story of a gifted orator who traveled throughout the Midwest for many years. This dynamic speaker would recite poems, scriptures, beautiful prose and other well-known readings in concert halls, schools and churches. He was widely respected for his wonderful sense of pacing, gestures, intonation and inflection as he recited by memory his entire presentations.

Word spread that this inspirational public speaker was going to address a gathering at a little church in a small town in Iowa. The Sunday evening finally arrived, and a standing room only crowd gathered to hear the famous orator.

For nearly two hours the rhetorician shared a spellbinding performance. He concluded his presentation by reciting the 23rd Psalm with great force and beauty. As he finished the final verse of the Psalm, the crowd burst into a massive standing ovation.

The orator then spoke to the gathering, saying, *"I'd like to ask the pastor of the church to conclude our presentation tonight by also reciting the 23rd Psalm."* The pastor was a simple man of faith, an immigrant who spoke in broken English, and he reluctantly came up to the pulpit, feeling insecure to follow such a gifted speaker. The pastor stumbled and mumbled his way through the 23rd Psalm, and when he concluded, there was no ovation. But, you could see tears of love coming from many who held great affection for this man who had served his congregation so faithfully for many years.

The orator stood up by the pastor, now putting his arm around him and said simply to the crowd, "I know the Psalm, but this man knows the Shepherd."

My goal in writing this chapter is to help each of us understand more deeply than ever before not only the 23rd Psalm, but more importantly, to come to know the Good Shepherd more intimately than ever before as He calls us to a life of joy and serenity.

The 23rd Psalm is used more often in hospitals, memorial services and in ministering to the bereaved and brokenhearted than any other passage in all of Scripture. Yet, in the familiarity it is easy for us to lose something of the profound significance of the passage. By way of background, two great truths may help us gain a deeper understanding of this Psalm and its timeless relevance for us today:

1. The Psalm is written from the viewpoint of the sheep.

Allegorically, it is the testimony of a four-footed animal. Spiritually, it is the testimony of a child of God, who is pictured again and again throughout Scripture as a sheep before his shepherd.

2. The first verse states the theme for the entire Psalm.

"The Lord is my shepherd, I shall not want." (Psalm 23:1) If we take this one sentence and work our way through the six verses, we will discover how this one great truth is deeply woven into the fabric of this Psalm: *"The Lord is my shepherd, I shall not want."*

For example, I shall not want for rest, or he makes me lie down (vs. 2). I shall not want for self-restoration, for He restores my soul (vs. 3). I shall not want for His love, for His goodness and mercy and loving kindness will follow me all the days of my life (vs 6). *"The Lord is my shepherd, I shall not want."*

John Linn was a loving teacher to children. His ministry was unique in all of Scandinavia as he traveled from church to church to minister not to adults or teenagers, but always to little children. John loved to teach children passages of the Bible, and often even the youngest of children were able to memorize sections of the Bible.

On one occasion, Linn had spent an entire week with a group of children in a small church, and on the last day of his ministry there, he asked during the Sunday morning service, "Would one of you children come forward in front of the congregation, and quote by memory the 23rd Psalm?"

At first, all of the children were nervous, and no child was willing to volunteer. Finally, a tiny four year old girl lifted her hand high, came forward, took a bow and said softly, *"The Lord is my Shepherd, He's all I want."* And then she sat down.

I'd suggest she said it all. I'd suggest this little girl had a wonderful grasp of the Psalm, for she stated very clearly the message of the 23rd Psalm: *"The Lord is our Shepherd, He's all we want."*

Or is He? If we are not careful, it's very easy for a pastor, a coach, a spouse, or a romantic partner to become our primary Shepherd. The Psalmist says, *"I have one Shepherd, and He is our loving God. He is the object of my greatest affection."*

Psalm 23:2 begins, *"He makes me lie down in green pastures."* For most of my life, I've thought the emphasis in this verse was on the "green pastures." In the original Hebrew text, however, the emphasis is not on the green pastures. The emphasis is on the verb: "He *makes* me lie down in green pastures."

As you know, there are other animals with more natural intelligence than sheep. Further, sheep tend to be defenseless. They have no great speed which enables them to race away from some treacherous animal such as a wolf. Also, they are easily fearful, so afraid that they fear noises. An unusual sound can cause the sheep to run in different directions, and frequently become lost in the thickets. Accordingly, it is often the task of the shepherd to take the sheep by the ears, and force their heads down until the sheep "lie down in green pastures." *"He makes me lie down in green pastures."*

How about us? Has our Good Shepherd *made* us lie in green pastures recently? In our hectic, hurried, harried pace, it becomes very easy for us to become anxious, worried, and stressed. So at times, it is necessary for our loving Shepherd to grab us by our spiritual ears, and make us lie down for a season of rest, renewal and serenity.

There are many ways He does this:

- Sometimes the way He makes us lie down in green pastures is when we lose a loved one by death, and we are reminded of the brevity of life that ultimately all that truly matters is our relationships: God, family, friends. All those material things we yearn to possess will have no eternal value.

- Sometimes the way He makes us lie down in green pastures is through a loved one who comes to us and says, "You are so busy making a living that we have no life together in our home, with our family."

- Sometimes the way He makes us lie down in green pastures is through a stress related illness that perhaps leaves us bed ridden for a time (86% of primary care physician visits are in some way stress related.)

There is a myriad of ways that the Good Shepherd uses to make us lie down in green pastures. And, not only does He lovingly do this for us, but He's also gracious enough to quiet the waters for us. The Hebrew text in Psalms 23:2 literally reads: *"He leads me beside waters of rest."* As you may know, sheep do not like for water to move in a fast current. Splashing water disturbs them. They perhaps fear, among other emotions, drowning. Their heavy wool coats are like sponges, and when they absorb water, the sheep can feel as though they will be pulled into the rapidly moving stream. In point of fact, they could easily suffocate in the water.

So the Shepherd will often pull some rocks from the side of the banks into a small area of the stream, and block a section of the stream so as to allow the sheep to drink in a calm setting. *"He leads me beside waters of rest."*

I've long believed that if we are to discover the green pastures and the still waters of life, there are three ingredients we must build into our lives with intentionality:

1. **A Sabbath**
2. **A Safe Place**
3. **Two or Three Safe Friends**

A Sabbath

We need to be certain that we have one day in every week for renewal, rest, prayer, play, laughter and loving relationship building. If it can't be one day, start with a few hours and build up to a full day. Author Wayne Muller writes, "To be unable to find time for the sunset, to whiz through our obligations without time for a single, mindful breath, this has become the model of a successful life. How have we allowed this to happen? This was not our intention, this is not the world we dreamed of when we were young and our whole life was full of possibility and promise. How did we get so terribly lost in a world saturated with striving and grasping, yet somehow bereft of joy and delight? 'Remember the Sabbath' means, remember that everything you have received is a blessing. Remember to delight in your life, remember to stop and offer thanks for the wonder of it all.'" How are we doing at honoring a Sabbath?

A Safe Place

It can be a room in your home, a favorite spot in nature, a path you walk every day, a bench at a lovely nearby park. It is a place to go to be alone with your dreams, your fears, your prayers, your tears, your joys. Because I live near the ocean, I have a special spot by a beach, and I go there alone to commune with God. How are we doing at spending time in a safe place?

Two or Three Safe Friends

When I lived in Minneapolis, I taught a class called *The 3 A.M. Christian* where together we discovered the ingredients of a friendship so compassionate, authentic and kind that if it was 3 a.m., and we couldn't sleep due to some unrelenting anxiety, we could call that "safe friend". How are we doing at developing two or three safe friends?

I have a hunch that we miss the green pastures and the still waters of Psalm 23 because we have no Sabbath, or no Safe Place, or no Safe Friends.

As we continue our reflections on this beloved Psalm, we must acknowledge that sheep can be very stubborn. Sheep are often determined to go their own way. As a matter of fact, perhaps the best description of our stubborn nature that we find in all of scripture is found in Isaiah 53:6 where we read, *"All we like sheep have gone astray. We have turned everyone to his own way."*

When we, like sheep, chose to go our own way, David tells us in Psalm 23 that we need to be restored. *"He restores my soul."* (Psalm 23:3)

Many Bible teachers have suggested that the primary meaning of this verse can be found in the truth that God seeks to encourage us when we are disheartened. Others suggest that the verse is teaching that the Good Shepherd is there to renew us in our weariness. We know both these thoughts are true because they are affirmed elsewhere in Scripture. But, the original Hebrew word translated into English as "restore" literally means, *"to turn around so as to rearrange one's life."* It is the picture of a sheep going one way into a thicket and the shepherd coming with his staff and turning the sheep around. It is the exact same concept that we find in the New Testament word spoken by Christ when He says, "Repent." The Greek term is "metanoia," and it clearly implies to turn around from disobedience to faithfulness.

In different areas of our lives, perhaps there are some of us who are choosing to go our own way. We may need the loving staff of the Good Shepherd to turn us around and enable us to get back on course.

The Psalm next guides us toward getting on the right course in Verse 3: "He leads me in the paths of righteousness for His name's sake." Before a watching world, God's name is at stake in our lives. It is for His name's sake that He turns our lives around. It is for His reputation that He seeks to restore us. *"He leads me in the path of righteousness for His name's sake."* All the glory for our lives of compassion go to Him.

Now, the tone of the Psalm changes. In verse 4, David begins to show us that the wonderful promises of God's provision and restoration must be lived out in the harsh realities of the real world. *"Though I walk through the valley of the shadow of death, I will fear no evil, for thou art with me."*

This verse is one of many that contains within it what I believe to be the central promise in all of scripture for the Christian as he lives out his life in the world: the promise of God's presence: "Thou art with me."

In Palestine, the shepherd leads his sheep in the winter months to the lowland areas. The highlands are too cold. But as the summer sun begins to melt away the freezing snow, the shepherd leads his sheep up into the fresh areas of green grass. That journey upward, as any mountain climber could tell you, is often treacherous. The shepherd leads his sheep up along the path, and it is a trail filled with difficulties and hardships. For some of the sheep, it is nothing less than *"the valley of the shadow of death."* I never find, throughout this Psalm or in any other section of scripture, that the Christian life is a life of ease. It is most unfortunate that we ever leave that impression in the life of someone who is considering the claims of Christ. At times, the

Christian life is a life in the valleys. At times, it is a life of dark shadows. At times, it is a life where death will have to be confronted in our own lives, or the life of a loved one. But the good Shepherd is with us. That's the promise of verse 4.

Please note: The verse does not say, "We might walk through the valley." It says, "even though we walk through the valley". The valleys will be there, but so will God, and his rod and staff will comfort us right in the middle of the valleys.

Psalm 23:5 has puzzled Bible students through the centuries. Verse 5 begins, *"Thou prepareth a table before me in the presence of my enemies. Thou anointest my head with oil."* I can still remember as a child hearing that verse, and picturing sitting around a dinner table with some people who didn't like me, a disgruntled classmate or a bully from school — and that somehow God had set up this table. What is David writing about here?

We must remember that this Psalm is written throughout from the perspective of a sheep. At this point in the Psalm, the Shepherd has led his sheep up those hazardous valleys, as he moves from the winter lowland to the spring high country. There the Shepherd is seeking what he knows by only one name: "The Tableland", often referred to as simply "The Table".

The tables are the plateaus in the foothills and mountains where fresh green grass is growing. It is a place of nourishment where the sheep can eat. The Shepherd goes before his sheep and prepares the table for the sheep. As he does so, he knows that the one key enemy of the sheep as he travels from the winter lowlands to the spring highlands is the snake who, in the hillsides of Palestine, tends to live in a hole in the ground.

The Shepherd knows the snake, then troubled by the movement of the sheep above him, will crawl quickly into a hole and then bite the sheep. So the wise and loving Shepherd goes ahead of his flock, and with his staff he moves the grass aside looking for the holes. When he finds one, he draws from his side a small leather pouch filled with oil. The oil has an unpleasant odor, and the Shepherd pours the oil all around the hole. This serves as a repellant to the snake.

The discerning Shepherd knows that he will miss finding some holes, and so he goes back to his flock and with the surplus oil, anoints the head of the sheep. Now the repellent oil keeps the snake from biting the sheep's face when he leans over to eat the grass on the tables. *"Thou prepareth a table before me in the presence of mine enemies, thou anointest my head with oil."*

Having prepared the tables, the Shepherd will now often draw water in a bucket from a well in the highlands. He knows there are not as many streams at this altitude. And so, the Shepherd would pour refreshing water into a cup, and the sheep would come and drink. *"My cup runneth over."*

When we look back and we see the faithfulness of The Good Shepherd in all these things, our testimony will be: *"Surely goodness and mercy shall follow me all the days of my life."*

As we conclude this chapter, affirm in your own heart the words of the 23rd Psalm with perhaps a deeper understanding and a more grateful heart than ever before:

> *"The Lord is my Shepherd; I shall not want. He maketh me lie down in green pastures: He leadeth me beside the still waters. He restoreth my soul: He leadeth me in the paths of righteousness for His name's sake. Yea, though I walk through the valley of the shadow of death, I will fear no evil for thou art with me. Thy rod and thy staff, they comfort me. Thou preparest a table before me in the presence of mine enemies: thou anoinest my head with oil; my cup runneth over. Surely goodness and mercy shall follow me all the days of my life; and I will dwell in the house of the Lord forever."*

Chapter 34

CHOOSING JOY AS WE HONOR OUR HIGHEST CALLING IN LIFE

"Now it came to pass, as they went, that He entered into a certain village: and a certain woman named Martha received Him into her house. And she had a sister called Mary, who sat at Jesus' feet, and heard His word. But Martha was distracted about much serving, and came to Him, and said, 'Lord, dost thou not care that my sister hath left me to serve alone? Tell her to help me.' And Jesus answered and said unto her, 'Martha, Martha, thou art troubled about many things: But one thing is needful: and Mary hath chosen that good part, which shall not be taken away from her.' " ~ Luke 10:38-42

Steven McDonald was a police officer working in New York City. One summer day Steven stopped to question a group of teenage boys regarding some stolen bicycles that McDonald was trying to retrieve. One of the fifteen year old boys in question pulled a handgun, and shot Steven in the head and the neck.

The shots paralyzed McDonald from the neck down through his entire body. Miraculously, Steven survived. He spent eighteen months in the hospital recuperating, and learning how to live as a quadriplegic.

At the time of the shooting, Officer McDonald had been married two years, and his wife was six months pregnant with their first child. Remarkably, Steven and his wife chose to reframe their thinking about this crime, with the help of God. Rather than focusing on all that had been taken away from them, they decided to focus all their combined energies into discovering what God's plan was for their future ministry together. They forgave the teenage boy who had shot McDonald, and who was now in prison. Several months later, the assailant called from prison to express his sorrow for his actions. Steven not only accepted his apology, but he also told the young man that he hoped one day they could travel the country together, sharing their story in high schools in hopes of preventing other acts of violence.

Officer McDonald never had the chance to live out this part of his dream, as three days after his assailant was released from prison, the young man was killed in a motorcycle accident. So Steven set out on his own to spread his message of forgiveness and reconciliation. He writes, *"The only thing worse than a bullet in my spine would have been to nurture revenge in my heart."*

Steven McDonald may have lost his physical mobility in the shooting, but he still had the power to transform his thinking with the help of God, and come to a place of inner peace and calm in his heart. In the process, Steven became a person with a Calling.

Discovering a spirit of calm in a chaotic world can be a challenge for each of us, especially if we are not focused on God's priorities for our lives. Several Christian psychologists have assisted us in our quest for self-understanding by drawing a distinction between a *driven* person and a *called* person.

While affirming that there can be a degree of overlap, in general terms, characteristics of a *driven* person would be as follows:

A Driven Person:

1. is most often gratified by accomplishments.
2. will often place a task ahead of a relationship.
3. is often abnormally busy.
4. tends to be extremely competitive.

By way of contrast, a *called* person is generally characterized as follows:

A Called Person:

1. has a clear sense of purpose.
2. sees the value of the person more than the task.
3. is so focused on his primary objectives that he is able to say "No" to secondary requests.
4. is able to balance diligent work with peaceful leisure.

Reflecting back over the past month, where would you place yourself in light of the preceding descriptions of a Driven Person in contrast to a Called Person?

In large measure, the way in which we respond to this question will determine the ways in which we will answer questions related to the issue of whether we are more like a Martha or more like a Mary in the touching, cherished story we read in Luke 10:38-42.

Tucked away in the pages of Luke's scroll is one of the most intimate vignettes we can ever read in all of the life of Christ. There is a home, located in a hamlet that rests two miles from the busy city of Jerusalem. The village is named Bethany, and the home in this tiny community is owned by Martha, the oldest of the three family members: Martha, Mary and Lazarus. Apparently all three of these siblings remained unmarried during the life and ministry of Jesus.

Christ chose their home as the place He would travel to for restoration, renewal and rest. It was His "safe place", His retreat center. Moving relentlessly toward the cross, Jesus must have looked forward with great anticipation to His sabbatical at the home of Martha, Mary and Lazarus. It was here where He could be with loved ones who had no hidden agenda, no leading questions, no ulterior motives. These were friends who loved him unconditionally.

A helpful question for us to ask ourselves as we reflect on this tender story from Luke 10 would be: *If Jesus physically lived on earth today, would He choose my home? Would He select my home or apartment as a place where He knew He could find rest, peace, compassion, kindness?*

As we gain an overview of both scripture and contemporary Christian psychology, we recognize that God has given a wide variety of temperaments to men and women. There are task-oriented Marthas. There are person-oriented Marys. Every temperament has flaws that if not yielded to God will seriously hinder that person's growth, ministry, family life and his or her own health. This reality is what will now be played out before us in this insightful account.

Luke doesn't waste time in his narrative in getting Jesus through the front door and into a conversation with Mary, who quickly seats herself at our Lord's feet. "After all," relationally-oriented Mary may be thinking to herself, "how often do we have this opportunity to sit and listen to The Master? Perhaps this will be one of the last times we will be with our Friend before the cross." Mary found great joy as she sat and interacted with Jesus, rather than being concerned with the physical needs and organizational tasks around the house.

The study in contrasts between Mary and Martha begins immediately in this passage. In fact, the very first time we read of Martha's response to Jesus coming to her home, we read that she is distracted. In the Greek text, the word we translate into English as "distracted" carries with it the idea of a divided mind. Martha has several things on her mind. She is task driven. She is the textbook first born, take-charge, organized child in this family.

Picture the scene with me. Martha is in the kitchen. She is working hard with the task of preparing the food. As her frustration with her sister grows, she finally stomps into the family room and says, in essence, *"Jesus, don't you care that Mary has left me to prepare the meal all alone? Tell her to help me!"*

As we gain an overview of scripture, we can affirm three statements regarding the anxiety that so often marks a person like Martha:

1. Anxiety highlights the human viewpoint and diminishes the Divine perspective.

2. Anxiety limits our ability to distinguish the incidental from the essential.
3. Anxiety robs us of our energy and joy.

Our hearts go out to Martha in compassion because we know she's just like us when we get our Eternal Priorities confused.

I've always loved Jesus' response to Martha's harsh confrontation. Christ replies, *"Martha, you are troubled and anxious about many things. Only one thing is needful."*

What's the "one thing?" A. T. Robertson writes wisely, *"Jesus could mean here 'just one dish, just a bowl of soup, just a loaf of bread, that's all, that's plenty.'"*

Jesus seems to be saying, in essence, *"Martha, what Mary has chosen won't be taken away from her. The food – we'll enjoy it, but then it's gone. The memory of our lives shared together — that can last forever."*

Two principles of application emerge:

1. A Called Person decisively plans times of rest, renewal and leisure.

Jesus honored this principle in today's scripture. We think our work is important, but it's not as important as the work that Christ had to accomplish. Yet, on a number of occasions in the Gospels, we read that Jesus took time for rest, renewal and leisure in order to gain perspective with loved ones that He might overcome the temptation to succumb to anxiety.

Have you ever observed that Jesus was never in a hurry? I'm in a hurry nearly every day. Not once do we read that Jesus was in a hurry. I believe that's because He was absolutely focused on His Calling. He was a Called Person.

2. A Called Person lives his or her life focused on those things that are Eternal.

That's the choice that Mary made on that day so long ago in Bethany.

One Christian author shares that after studying this passage he offered the following prayer:

> *"Heavenly Father, if I'm candid, I'd have been Martha, not Mary. And I know that my task orientation can be a good and helpful temperament for Your Kingdom. But, help me to commit myself from this day forward to investing my life in people, and only in those things that are Eternal. Amen."*

And what are the things that are Eternal? As I've noted before, I believe there are only two:

1. Our relationship with God.
2. Our relationship with people.

Everything else will pass away! Accordingly, our hearts as Called People need to be set everyday on these two relationships.

Next to the Bible, the book that has most deeply influenced my life is *The Seven Habits of Highly Effective People* by Steven Covey. I have read, and re-read it scores of times. One of the seven habits that Covey challenges us to build into our character is: *"Begin with the end in mind.* As Christians, I believe we are to begin each day with this great end in mind: *There are only two things that are going to last forever: our relationship with God, and our relationships with people, especially the loved ones in our care.* So we want to be certain that we are investing our lives every day in our relationship with God, and our relationships with people. That is what it means to be a Called Person!

Dorothea Clapp invested her life in her relationship with God, and her relationship with people. In the 1950's, Mrs. Clapp used to pray daily for the young students in her Sunday School class in her hometown of Ramsey, New Jersey. Throughout her life, Dorothea distributed Bible tracts in the train station, worked with a youth Bible Club in her poor neighborhood, taught Sunday School, and led scores of children, youth and adults to Christ. She always gave 50% of her meager income to support her church, and other missionaries to the poor around the world.

In 1952, Dorothea sensed that God had especially placed on her heart a teenager named George Verwer. She prayed daily for George, she reached out to him and built a deep, loving relationship with him. In time, she felt led to give him the Gospel of John, as George had no background in knowing who Jesus was. And then one night, she led him to Christ.

As Dorothea continued to invest her life in George Verwer, this young man's heart began to grow in his absolute passion for Christ. Soon he would found an organization called *Operation Mobilization*. *Operation Mobilization* grew to train hundreds of mission workers spreading the Gospel, and ministering to the poor in some of the most hardened and seemingly impenetrable countries in the world.

In November of 1989, at the age of 88, Dorothea Clapp passed from this life into Eternity. But she lives on in two ways: she lives on forever with Christ, and she lives on in the lives of scores of people all around the world. Dorthea Clapp found joy and meaning in her life by honoring her highest calling. Do you? Do I?

☙

ACKNOWLEDGEMENTS

"A man ought to so live that everyone knows he is a Christian, and most of all, his family ought to know."
Dwight L. Moody

My beloved father, Reverend D. C. Davis, served his God faithfully throughout his life. During his 25-year ministry at Westminster Presbyterian Church in Clarinda, Iowa, my dad led a vital and dynamic ministry with children and youth. Young people were attracted to his gentleness, kindness, joy and unconditional love.

During his years in Clarinda, my father initiated a ministry called *Begin the Week with God*. The format was simple: a light breakfast held in the church basement, dad sharing a brief devotional, and a time of prayer for each other as we began a new week. Young people came from other churches for the Monday morning breakfast, and many high school students who had no church home joined in as well. Everyone was welcome.

Several years ago, I began to write a weekly column entitled *Begin the Week with God* in honor of my father. These columns were well received by readers around the United States and globally. Many of the columns serve as the foundation of the chapters in this book.

Stacy Madden, my long-time friend and a devoted Christian, provided invaluable support, guidance and insight throughout the development of this book including art direction, cover design, editing, project management, and marketing.

My friend, Joanne Holdsworth Bouslough, tirelessly edited and refined this book, graciously extending abundant amounts of time, and unwavering devotion and loyalty.

Two beloved friends — Dr. Gene Lucas, Professor and Executive Vice Chancellor Emeritus, University of California, Santa Barbara; and Peggy Schierl, retired counselor with Masters degrees in Theology and Counseling — both offered their indispensable wise insights and perspectives to the content of this book.

Much of the content of this book was discussed and refined by a small group of Christian friends who met with me weekly: Dave and Bonnie Schreiner, Ann and Rudy Aguilera, Janet Seaboyer, and Don and Judy Nason. I am grateful for their kindness and wisdom.

Many authors have profoundly influenced me in shaping my understanding of joyful living and healthy aging. These include: Dr. Dean Ornish, Henri Nouwen, J. Keith Miller, Bruce Larson, Albert Schweitzer, John Robbins, Phillip Keller, Joan Borysenko, Kelly McGonigal, Douglas Lisle, Dr. Michael Greger, Dr. Garth Davis, Charles Swindoll, Steven Covey, Elizabeth Elliott, Dr. Martin Seligman, Gretchen Rubin, Dietrich Bonhoeffer, Dr. Neil Barnard, Dr. Joel Furham, Tim Hansel, Brendon Burchard, Sara Gottfied, Dr. T. Colin Campbell, Dan Buettner, Dr. Andrew Weil, and Dr. Wayne Muller.

Finally, my children, Rachael and Nathan, have come alongside me throughout this precious life journey, and have taught me so much about choosing joy. Their unconditional love and unfailing support have emboldened me to write this book. Being a father to Rachael and Nathan has brought untold joy and meaning to my life. The impact of their lives is found throughout *Choosing Joy: The Pathway to a Life of Passion and Purpose.*

www.ingramcontent.com/pod-product-compliance
Lightning Source LLC
LaVergne TN
LVHW011217080426
835509LV00005B/167